Pascal's
Lettres Provinciales

Pascal's
Lettres Provinciales

The Motif and Practice
Of Fragmentation

by

Louis A. MacKenzie, Jr.

SUMMA PUBLICATIONS, INC.
Birmingham, Alabama
1988

ISBN 0-917786-63-7
Library of Congress Catalog Number 88-61122

Printed in the United States of America

For JoAnn and Ian

Contents

Foreword

IN LIGHT OF THEIR TEXTUAL FRAGMENTATION, which is also their mystery, the *Pensées* have been easily and permanently adopted by modern thought, tastes, and critical dispositions. Their attractiveness is due, at least in part, to the fact that the purely theological aspects are complemented by, and filtered through, psychological, metaphysical, rhetorical, and stylistic considerations that form an essential part of the argument of the work. Moreover, the textual disorderliness of the *Pensées* allows for and encourages a certain latitude in reading them. The *Provinciales,* Pascal's other great work, and the one for which he was most celebrated in the seventeenth century (after his identity as author of the *petites lettres* had become known), are, in a sense, a more troublesome work for literary scholars; not because they are textually more difficult, but, rather, because they are more obvious and more baldly theological. While it is, of course, true that they may be approached from some of the same angles as the *Pensées,* the fact that they wear their theology very much on their sleeve tends to send many modern readers scurrying for the *Pensées*.

I make this point neither to cast aspersions nor to trumpet my own choice of material, but simply to situate myself in relation to the text I examine. This situating is, I believe, important when dealing with a work such as the *Provinciales* in which the author takes definite, and not always uncontroversial, positions with regard to the Catholic religion and religious truth. What is more, in as much as the *Provinciales* were intended to sway readers towards fundamentalist positions, or to further valorize those positions, and, since Pascal's argumentative voice is so dominant in the text, it is not always easy or convenient to treat this work with obvious neutrality. In examining Pascal's conceptions of truth, for example, it may be necessary to refer, as does the author, to the terrible attack on that truth by the Jesuits. To make such references does not, however, imply that the critic has taken sides against the Jesuits, that Pascal has a proprietary hold on truth, or that Calvinists are heretics and that casuists are demonic.

What I am getting at in a rather roundabout way is simply this: my study of the *Provinciales* has tried to stick as resolutely as possible with what actually appears on the page of Pascal's text. I have tried to refrain from judgment on the issues, as issues. When I examine some of the casuist maxims on ethics, I examine them from the point of view of a reader of literature, not as an ethicist or a theologian. So my own discussion of truth in the *Provinciales* is a nonjudgmental one and is given the same emphasis as, say , a discussion of the principal image or structure in a more purely fictional work. Finally, and by the same token, the matter of fragmentation, which in the *Pensées* has clear structural and "theoretical" value, is, in the work I consider, Pascal's only finished piece of writing, more a thematic preoccupation.

In the study that follows, I consider the issue of fragmentation as fundamental to the problem that Pascal attacks as polemicist and as public relations manager of Port-Royal's cause. In a first section, I look at the current of quantification that in the argument Pascal advances would characterize Molinist thinking. In that argument, quantification and numerology would be given frequent privilege by the Molinists over the essential spirit of theological positions and liturgical practice held as sacred and immutable by the Jansenists. My second chapter will discuss the fragmentational linguistics and rhetoric of the Molinists. Once again, basic values such as words themselves as well as the social economy built around them would, in the polemic Pascal directs against his adversaries, be subjected to fragmentational tampering. A third chapter will discuss some of the activities by means of which Pascal is able to fragment the fragmentation of his adversaries. In a fourth and final section, I excavate some of the constituants of Pascal's organizational principle. This principle, Truth, would by definition be simple, immutable, and resistant to the ravages of novelty, relativism, and the fragmentational activity championed by the "modern" theologians whom Pascal targets mercilessly, but, to hear him tell it, "charitably" in these *petites lettres*.

Acknowledgment

The author gratefully acknowledges assistance from the Institute for Scholarship in the Liberal Arts, University of Notre Dame.

Chapter 1

By the Numbers: Quantification
And Numerologic in the *Provinciales*

THE *LETTRES PROVINCIALES* were an explosive work. Their explosiveness resides as much in their intent as in their timing.[1] According to the Jesuit chronicler and rhetorician René Rapin, the *Provinciales* represented such a fundamental mutation of method that Port-Royal was able to rise Phoenix-like from its ashes:

> A la vérité cette censure, toute autorisée qu'elle fut... n'eut pas l'effet qu'on s'en étoit promis, et l'on s'étonnera peut-être comment il s'est pu faire qu'un party qui venoit d'être si solennellement condamnée à Rome par le pape, que le clergé de France venoit de proscrire, la Sorbonne de censurer [...] ait non seulement trouvé moyen de subsister parmi tant de disgrâce, mais même soit en quelque façon devenu plus célèbre par ses propres ruines et faisant plus de bruit qu'il n'avoit encore fait: ce qui se fit aussy par une conduite la plus fine et la plus artificieuse qui fût jamais, par une méthode tout opposée à celle qu'on avait tenue.[2]

The disruption of stylistic and discursive norms that Rapin is obliged to admire, if in a begrudging way, is quite specifically at the bottom of the task facing Pascal. When, in the face of mounting pressure against Port-Royal, Antoine Arnauld appealed to Pascal's youthfulness, he was appealing to boldness, innovation, and cleverness—qualities that had already made Pascal a celebrity in the world outside of Port-Royal. The young scientist, mathematician, and inventor understood that if the pressures bearing on Port-Royal were to be vented, he would have to reorient the boundaries and operative terms of a dispute that had already been simmering in one form or another for some ninety years.[3] In taking up the cause, Pascal will do more than accuse. Arnauld's own tact had been accusatory—heartfelt, courageous, but in the end, ineffective. The reorientatiaon envisaged by Pascal would, in a manner of speaking, be vivisectional. The writer of the *Lettres* would make incursion into the workings, into the vital innards of what the Jansenists are convinced is a monstrous organism devouring the Church and its traditions from the inside. So Pascal, in the person of his fictional agent, Montalte, will get inside—or, more precisely, will give the impression of having recently found his way inside—the logic of Molinist thinking and teachings. From that vantage, he will show this thinking to be basically, even freakishly, illogical—and not just in its forms, but in its intent and consequences. In the view Pascal needs to put across, Molinist thinking would be dominated by an agenda of conceptual and practical fragmentation that will touch not only upon liturgical practice and ethical prescription, but on fundamental aspects of language itself.

Pascal's vivisectional activity will oblige him to do more than simply examine from a safe distance the living, two-headed creature called Molinism and casuistry; it will require him to cut it apart, to analyze and display its parts. In performing his analytical tasks, Pascal will allow the various elements of the system he cuts apart to thrash about on his operating table—on the page of his letter—where they, and the system from which they issue, are, at least in principle, destined to expire.[4]

Before looking at a first aspect of Pascal's activity, namely, his attention to the logic of quantification, it might be well to recall briefly the historical and ideological context in which that activity is situated. In the early 1640s, Corneille Jansen's *Augustinus* started making waves in the theological capitals of Europe. This weighty and, as subsequent controversy over textual evidence was to show, unwieldy book presumed to settle once and for all the nettlesome mystery of the interface between man's supposedly free will and God's all-powerful will. In espousing the letter and nuance of Augustine's thinking on these issues, Jansen's text flew directly in the face of some prevailing ideological winds. The stiffest of these had come from the South: Molinism, named after the Spanish Jesuit, Luis Molina, proposed what today might be called user-friendly attitudes on the relationship between human behavior, divine action, and ultimate rewards or punishments. In this system, it is argued that man's good works could bear directly on his prospects for salvation. According to the

Augustinian argument, however, salvation is an exclusively divine prerogative. In light of an original fall from grace, man could play but a minimal
part in his own eschatological fortunes. The particular pressures of the
Counter-Reformation rendered such divergent views of the human condition
all the more critical, especially when the Jansenist position could, without
too much gerrymandering, be interpreted as dangerously close to
Calvinism, that is, to heresy. Jansen's book was subjected to bristling
attack from the Jesuit camp at the University of Louvain and, in sermons
requisitioned by Richelieu himself, from the pulpit at Notre-Dame de Paris.
These attacks begged—and begot—response from the Jansenist brain trust.
The most important of these responses came from the quill of Antoine
Arnauld. In his *Apologie pour Jansenius* and *De la fréquente communion,*
Arnauld targets specific doctrinal questions, while in collaboration with
François Hallier, later to take up the Jesuit side, he engages in a frontal
maneuver against his Jesuit adversaries by exposing the principles and
practices of their teachings on ethics.

On the strictly dogmatic issues, the debate focused on what were to
become commonly known as the five propositions. Originally seven in
number, these propositions, purportedly gleened from recent dissertations at
the Sorbonne, were to be scrutinized by the house theologians. As was
evident to anyone intimate with the larger political and ideological lines of
the controversy, the *mise en cause* of the propositions was but a thinly
cloaked attack against Jansenius's book specifically and Augustinism
generally; and if the objective of the controversy was clear enough, the
object itself was marked by ambiguity, imprecision, and bias. As one
specialist puts it, the heresy or orthodoxy of the propositions was fairly well
in the eyes, heart, and predisposition of the beholder:

> Coupées comme elles sont de leur contexte, ces propositions sont
> susceptibles d'une interprétation orthodoxe autant que d'une interpré-
> tation hérétique; de là la possibilité de puiser dans l'*Augustinus* cinq
> phrases textuellement contraires aux propositions condamnées.[5]

Despite the dauntest efforts by the Jansenist elite, the propositions were
condemned some four years after their publication by the papal bull *Cum
occasione;* and while the Jansenists deferred in public to Rome's jurisdiction
on the theological admissibility of the propositions as expressed out of
context, they demurred at admitting that this version faithfully represented
Jansen's intent. For their part, the Molinists saw in Rome's condemnation

de facto authorization to take a different path—the low road; and in the months following the papal pronouncement, a number of calumnious anti-Jansenist tracts were put into circulation. During this period, each side held fast regarding the propositions, and what Voltaire was to call the "guerre de plume" exploded in full fury. The wordy warriors shelled each other with libels and letters; and the Jansenists, already losing ground on most fronts, were ambushed in the confessional. The *affaire picoté,* named after the prelate at Saint-Sulpice who refused absolution to the Marquis de Liancourt, a Jansenist sympathizer, triggered a major escalation of hostilities. Indeed, it henceforth became fashionable to consider the Jansenists as patently heretical.

    In his two public letters of 1655, Arnauld had to respond to this most serious of accusations; and if these texts ("Lettre à une personne de qualité" and the "Seconde lettre à un duc et pair") highlight his eloquence, they also mark him as an increasingly ineffective spokesman for Port-Royal's cause. One historian puts it this way:

> "Ce qui n'appartient qu'à M. Arnauld" pour reprendre l'expression si juste de Vincent de Paul, c'est cette manie d'ergoter, d'entreprendre des discussions interminables [...]. Et tandis que, par des *distinguos* subtils, il pense avoir désarmé ses adversaires, voici que, inhabile à cet art de l'équivoque, inapte à ces retractions incessantes, par lesquelles Saint-Cyran se dérobait aux coups dont il se sentait menacé, il laisse échapper des phrases trop nettes, des arguments sur le sens duquel aucune ambiguité n'est possible et dont le retentissement l'étonne. Merveilleuse machine à syllogismes, mais fonctionnant souvent à vide, incapable en tout cas de cet effort de sympathie qui peut seul nous donner le sens de la pensée d'autrui [...].[6]

Louis Cognet puts it more succinctly in the introduction to his edition of the *Provinciales:* "Port-Royal abondait en théologiens, mais manquait de publicistes."[7] And in the face of the gloomy storm clouds gathering at the Sorbonne signaling the imminent censure of Arnauld, a publicist was precisely what was needed. Port-Royal's publicist was, of course, Blaise Pascal, who in January 1656 started turning out a series of letters which collectively would come to be called the *Provinciales*. It would not be too much of an exaggeration to regard the publication of these *petites lettres,* as they were called at the time, as a major media event. Concocted in secret and printed clandestinely, they quickly became the talk of town, gown, and province. That talk was a direct function of the daring and innovative rhetorical strategies adopted by Pascal.

Now, while the letter was not an uncommon vehicle for debate; and while Arnauld himself had turned to the epistolary form in defense of his positions, such letters were either patently public or voluminous affairs. The *Provinciales* were of an altogether different stamp: at least up through Letter 10 they had the feel of private correspondence, which, even though circulating in public, were designed to give the reader a sense of having gotten hold of something destined for other hands. This imparted a special savor to the reception of the material contained in the letters. Masked and attenuated in this illusion of intimate correspondence is the kind of obvious public posturing that might have detracted from the success of the letters, a success attributable in large part to Pascal's aggressive adherence to the principle of *agrément,* itself linked to the art of persuasion. One of the most basic components of this *agrément*—a term that points at once to the agreableness or pleasure imbedded in the text and to the resulting assent or agreement of the pleased reader—is the solidarity the writer/"sender" of the letters is able to establish right from the start with that reader.

The first letter, the one that burst onto the scene from out of nowhere, begins with the word "Monsieur." It has been argued that this *monsieur* is, in fact, Florin Perrier, Pascal's brother-in-law; and so he may be, but this need not—and cannot—rule out consideration of the broader public presumed in the word. At the very minimum, "monsieur" is the equivalent of "to whom it may concern"—or perhaps more precisely, "to him who may be concerned by what is going on." From this angle, "monsieur" is the one whose concern is to be curried and amplified. This concern will derive from sympathy, which itself derives from knowledge. For the writer of the *Letters,* the first order of business has to be a dispelling of ignorance, which will then allow for the establishment of a proper footing with his reader. In anticipation of the analytical operations to follow, that footing will be based on the letter writer's enlightenment and consequent self-assurance in the face of "obscure" goings on at the Sorbonne. The sense of solidarity that Pascal establishes with his reader at the outset of his first letter serves not only as backdrop to the rhetorical exigencies of the task before him, but also as the conceptual and ideological underpinning of that task. On both accounts, Pascal is moved to establish his credibility, his veracity, and his distance from error. And it is this that he needs to share with his reader; it is in this that he wants his reader, this "monsieur," to participate. When Louis de Montalte, Pascal's fictional investigative reporter, comes from nowhere to point out the naked truth under the emperor's new clothes, he would at once exile ignorance and error to an indefinite past and put into place the first links of something like an intelligence network.

> "Je ne suis détrompé que d'hier; jusqu'à là j'ai pensé que le sujet des disputes de Sorbonne était bien important, et d'une conséquence pour la religion. Tant d'assemblées d'une compagnie aussi célèbre qu'est la faculté de théologie de Paris, et où il s'est passé tant de choses si hors d'exemple, en font concevoir une si haute idée qu'on ne peut croire qu'il n'y ait un sujet bien extraordinaire."[8]

In this opening moment of the argument, Montalte explains why his error, now corrected, was in fact reasonable. As anyone might have done, he too had been distracted by the display of so much activity at the Sorbonne. As anyone might have done, he could not help but imagine a functional relationship between a frenzy of activity and the seriousness of the questions being debated.

By underscoring the normalcy and the logic of his reaction, he continues to forge with his reader an alliance based on "misconceptions" that they logically hold in common. Simultaneous to this provisional and calculated deflation of the narrator's and the reader's savvy is a relentless rhetorical inflation of the causes of deception. In the same way that he moves from what would be the "bien important sujet des disputes" to a more exaggerated expression—"extrême conséquence pour la religion"—he distends the reader's preconceptions by pumping into them a sequence of quantitative expressions: "tant d'assemblées"; "tant de choses si extraordinaires et si hors d'exemple"; "une si haute idée"; "sujet bien extraordinaire." From a phonological perspective, one can see—or hear—in the obvious insistence on sibilants, an object being inflated to the bursting point; the object in this case being both the reader's credulity and the Sorbonne's credibility. The explosion primed in this section comes in the succeeding paragraph, which too is charged with sibilants: "Cependant vous serez bien surpris quand vous apprendrez, par ce récit, à quoi se termine un si grand éclat; et c'est ce que je vous dirai en peu de mots, après m'en être parfaitement instruit" (Letter 1, p. 35). This "grand éclat"—on the one hand the fireworks display at the Sorbonne, and on the other, the display itself detonating under the pressure of Pascal's rhetorical sabotage—is put into particular relief by its own phonological signature, specifically in the repetition of the explosive phoneme [p] that punctuates the sibilants.[9] In effect, Pascal's rhetorical charge fragments what he had initially characterized as the undefined and indefinitely recurring events at the Sorbonne into "peu de mots," and eventually into two questions, "l'une de fait; l'autre de droit."

The signal Pascal wants to send at the outset is that the forces swirling around Arnauld and the Augustinian principles he champions are marked by frantic multiplication and inflation.[10] The aptness of this opening signal becomes even clearer to the reader who, as he moves through the *Provinciales,* will be confronted with more and more evidence of a Molinist logic based on quantitative or numerological factors. Indeed, Pascal will put great stock in the notion that the Jesuits have sold out principle in the name of theo-political objectives grounded ostensibly in the quantitative. "Il n'importe quelles tables de Jésus-Christ soient remplies d'abominations, pourvu que vos églises soient pleines de monde" (Letter 16, p. 222). And in order that *their* churches (Pascal's use of the possessive underscores his conviction that the Jesuits do not represent the true sense of *the* Church) be full of "clients," the casuists' manuals will have to be full of maxims capable of adjudicating the cases of an infinitely large population. The point is made in Letter 8: "On ne saurait, [...] écrire pour trop de monde, ni particulariser trop les cas, ni répéter trop souvent les mêmes choses en différents livres" (Letter 8, p. 120).

In his counter-fragmentational analysis of their positions and presuppositions, Pascal will virtually thematize the Jesuits' investment in the logic of numbers and quantity. It is perhaps important to recall, if only in a parenthetical way, that Pascal and his collaborators already know what and whom Port-Royal is up against. Unlike the fictional Montalte, the equally fictional provincial reader and, one can presume, a certain number of actual readers—all participants in the "discovery" of the truth as it unfolds in the *Lettres*—the Jansenist polemicists are already keenly aware of the character of their adversaries' alliances and arguments. To inflict as much damage as possible, while at the same time avoiding the kind of abstract dogmatism that had characterized earlier Jansenist riposts, Pascal will launch a multilayered rhetorical attack designed to strike his adversaries—and his readers' fancy—at/on a number of points. Figuring among these points is the one we are in the process of investigating, namely, numerology. Now, this aspect, perceived by the Jansenists as correlative to the political, moral, and theological positions of their adversaries, will, as mentioned earlier, appear in the *Provinciales* as something analagous to a theme in a purely literary text; and at the risk of digressing too far from the questions at hand, or of belaboring what may seem evident, it should be emphasized that attention to the "literary" or thematic ingredients of the *Provinciales* does in no way refute their circumstantial origin or their nonfictional musculature. On the other hand, a "literary" approach to the *Lettres* does not necessarily presuppose a detailed master scheme guiding the overall sequence of their production. It is obvious that for all their inventiveness, the *Provinciales* are not wholly a "creative" work. They are a hybrid in which fictive and factual simmer together in a way that allows for a variety of readings. To read the *Lettres* as one reads a literary text is in no way to demean their theological and historical features. It means, rather, that a spotlight has been trained upon particular aspects in order to illuminate their expression and deployment in the larger context of a work with evident literary qualities.

The numerological bias for which Pascal takes his adversaries to task, and at which he hints in the opening lines of the *Provinciales,* becomes explicit later on in the first letter. During the course of a discussion—a term I use in the strong sense of a shaking out—of the legitimacy of the expression "pouvoir prochain," the reader is presented with the following example of Molinist logic: "vous le direz [pouvoir prochain] ou vous serez hérétique, et M. Arnauld aussi, car nous sommes le plus grand nombre; et, s'il est besoin, nous ferons venir tant de Cordeliers que nous l'emporterons" (Letter 1, p. 42). The crucial word here is, of course, "car." This term establishes an intimate and "logical" relationship between the numerical supremacy of the Molinists and the promotion of questionable language into the lexicon of orthodoxy. The correctness of the terminology is to be guaranteeed neither by accepted use in theological discourse nor by magisterial decree from appropriate Church authority. Its correctness is to be guaranteed, as its use is to be obliged, by mere force of number.[11]

Pascal will insist on the importance of this numero-logic by having his fictional Molinists supplement what had just been presented as conclusive: should the "logic" of "le plus grand nombre" somehow fail to convince, an innumerable, and thus seemingly sufficient number of reserve troops—Franciscan monks—would be called up for active duty. It might be noted that if the words Pascal gives to the characters in the play he writes are exaggerated, they are not wholly contrived. In an account of the debate leading to the censure and expulsion of Arnauld, the Jansenist chronicler, Saint-Gilles, records the following:

> Le lendemain 16 Docteurs opinerent dont quatre seulement pour M. Arnauld. Il est remarquable que parmi les 12 autres il y avait sept Cordeliers, ce qui est une injustice notoire contre les statuts de la Faculté et contre les arrêts du Parlement, comme il a été dit; ces sortes de gens étant dans un tel dérèglement qu'ils sont les plus opposés (avec les Jésuites) à tout ce qui est ou approche du vrai bien.[12]

For Saint-Gilles, chronicler, factual details are going to matter a great deal; for Pascal, campaign manager and polemicist faced with a deteriorating situation, a certain latitude with the facts seems perfectly in order. The question does, however, remain open as to whether or not this sort of exaggeration and fictionalizing represent fraud, or if they simply provide a quicker cut to the larger issue of a court with a hostile claque.

By pointing to the defective "logic" of numbers, which he ironically refers to as the "solide raison" of the anti-Jansenist argument, Pascal puts into question not only the good faith of Arnauld's adversaries, but also their ability to fight a fair fight. He drives the point home all the more gleefully by having the Dominicans answer *en chœur*—"il faut, me dirent-ils tous ensemble, dire que tous les justes ont le pouvoir prochain." This is the knee-jerk response of someone backed into a corner by stronger argument and whose only recourse, short of admitting error, is to a boisterous and inflexible group response. In arranging a sectarian reaction having no discursive muscle, by having this wing of the opposition show a united front, Pascal in effect fragments the intended strength of that front by leading his readers to deduce that unity in error underscores disunity in fact. He further punctuates the falseness of the Molinist front by publicizing the matter of the half-hour of sand allotted to each speaker. For Montalte, this quantitative innovation, designed expressly to fragment the debate at the Sorbonne by limiting substantially the possibility of a proper defense on the part of Arnauld and his supporters, points eloquently to the shallowness and weak foundation upon which the case against Arnauld would be based. Indeed, Pascal underscores the detrimental effect of this quantification by pointing out that in artificially cutting ideas down to size—"taille-t-on vos avis à une certaine mesure?"—the position of the ignorant, that is of the Thomists and the other Molinist forces, is enhanced. Having virtually no time to enter into the substance of the issues, the ignorance and illogic of

the anti-Jansenist speakers will be less evident: "O la bonne règle pour
les ignorants! O l'honnête prétexte pour ceux qui n'ont rien à dire" (Letter
2, p. 45). For his part, the reader is becoming solidly familiarized with
the notion that the Molinists turn regularly to questionable tactics of
quantification. This is further confirmed in Letter 3 where Pascal points out
that the Jansenists have been submitted to a veritable litany of accusations
whose supposed persuasiveness would reside more in a quantitative
accumulation of such tactics than in properly informed and formed
argument.[13]

The spectacular success of the first letter, justifying as it does his
choice of subjects and approach, will encourage Pascal to continue down a
similar discursive path. Over the course of the *Provinciales,* he will
continue, then, to needle the Molinists for their subscription to quantifica-
tional modes of thinking, and will succeed in impressing upon his readers
the idea that such modes of thought are indeed characteristic of his adversaries. For example, in Letter 4 where Pascal first targets the Jesuits by
name, the matter of quantification is given special emphasis. The immediate
controversy revolves around the Jesuit pretense that an action cannot be
considered sinful when there has been no prior divine intervention
informing the would-be sinner of the evil he is about to commit, thus giving
him the means to avoid it. Montalte, completely taken aback ("étonné") by
what seems to him a categorical preclusion of sins of surprise as well as
those committed in total neglect of God, insists that his Jesuit informant
furnish textual proof that *grâce actuelle* is indeed a tenet of his order's
theology. Rising to the task, the good father heads out to the library for the
appropriate tomes. This hiatus gives Montalte and his Jansenist companion
occasion to discuss the likely character of the texts to which they are about
to be submitted. The Jansenist is already convinced that patristic, papal, or
scriptural precedent will not figure in the criteria by which the books are to
be evaluated. What will matter, rather, will be their alignment with casuist
thinking—and the weight of their numbers: "il vous en emportera beau
nombre." Since Pascal is pulling all the strings here, the reference to the
quantity of casuist texts is a significant detail. The issue is not only the
material contained in those texts, nor the proliferation of that material; it is
also the argument that would derive from that proliferation. The texts are
numerous, *therefore* there must be value to the material they contain. The
argument is, of course, specious, but that is precisely the point Pascal wants
to make. It is hardly a surprise that the Jesuit returns to center stage "chargé

de livres." The reader can easily visualize the good-hearted, but simple-minded, cleric teetering under the burden of his books—books which, over the course of the *Provinciales,* Pascal will try to render as burdensome as possible to those who subscribe to them.

Since from the Jansenist perspective these books represent a sabotaging of the foundations of the Church itself, Pascal sees to it that the first casuist text mentioned is one bearing a title especially useful to that perspective. As the Jesuit tenders this *Somme des péchés,* he expresses his admiration for the book and gives as warrant of its worth the fact—which he proclaims proudly—that it is in its fifth press run: "Lisez, me dit-il, la *Somme des péchés* du Père Bauny, que voici, et de la cinquième édition encore, pour vous montrer que c'est un bon livre." This remark serves Pascal's designs in several ways: not only does it further establish in the reader's mind the numerological mindset of the Jesuits, it also wants to show them as brazen and self-satisfied in their defective patterns of thought.

Montalte's Jansenist companion counters the Jesuit's logic of quantification with an argument based on substance: he refers to the book's content. Indeed, he is quick to inform Montalte—and the readers of the letter—that the book has already been condemned in Rome and in France. Pascal's reorienting of Jesuit numerologic back into the discourse of substance is punctuated by his exploitation of François Hallier's caricature of the author of the *Somme des péchés* as "he who takes away the sins of the world." That this remark is attributable to a former adversary turned ally of the Jesuits is doubly useful to the author of the *Provinciales.* He benefits, on the one hand, from the corrosive precision of Hallier's irony; and on the other, he can let the remark subtend his own charge of a usurpation of Church tradition, since in the standard use of the phrase, it is Jesus Christ himself, the "Lamb of God," not Etienne Bauny, who is said to take away the sins of the world.

The forceful discursive status afforded to quantitative thinking is reiterated in the seventh letter. Pascal's Jesuit puppet has just promised to explain procedures for legalization of what would otherwise have been taken for violent crime. Feigning incredulity—which is a double incredulity since he is only pretending not to believe in order to get his Jesuit to utter what is substantively unbelievable—Montalte basically says "this I've got to see." (What actually appears on the page is: "Mais, mon Père, pour vous dire la vérité, je me défie un peu de vos promesses; et je doute que vos auteurs en disent autant que vous... "). The Jesuit riposte: "vous me faites tort; je n'avance rien que je ne prouve et par tant de passages, que leur nombre, leur autorité et leurs raisons vous rempliront d'admiration" (Letter 7, p. 98). The terms Pascal puts in his Jesuit's mouth, and the order in which they appear, are telling. The privilege he gives to manifestly quantitative language ("tant de passages," "leur nombre") serves essentially to ironize and devalue the "autorité" and the "raison" of these texts, precisely because the Jesuit would claim to prove the points he makes by turning—by having to turn—to a multiplicity of texts. The authority and correctness of these texts and of the positions they "prove," are then understood as the semantic equivalents of force and rationalization, both false premises in Pascal's argument.

Pascal's insistence on the argument of quantity, or rather, his persistence in laying that argument at the feet of his Jesuit adversaries, is geared to provide the reader with a sense of the foolishness and illogic of Jesuitical modes of thought. Among the points Pascal wants his reader to deduce is this: the naive argument of the Jesuit doubtless points to equally defective formulations on the substantive issues. This is certainly the sense one gets when Pascal attacks the Jesuit modifications of religious practice. These modifications are, in Pascal's argument, coextensive with the policy of serving the greatest possible number of souls, a policy that the letter writer identifies and isolates as exclusively statistical, quantitative, and political. Now, the stubborn pursuit of their demographic objectives has obliged the Jesuits to engage in an ongoing policy of experimentation and adjustment in order to entice and appease those with an appetite for less onerous spiritual responsibilities. To this end, two principal activities on the liturgical agenda, namely the sacrament of penance and the Mass itself, are rendered more palatable by treating them as divisible or quantifiable entities.

Pascal takes some pain to expose the "adoucissements de la Confession," which he esteems to be "le meilleur moyen que les pères aient trouvé pour attirer tout le monde et ne rébuter personnne" (Letter 10, p. 134). The Jesuit puppet is made to flaunt his Society's success at rendering inoffensive "un grand nombre de choses" that used to be considered sinful. He has to admit, however, that this policy has been but partially effective, and that a number of acts remain stubbornly imputable. For this a simple remedy has been devised, a remedy that would fundamentally alter the way the penitent views the sacrament. Since, in the view Pascal ascribes to the Jesuits, one of the penitent's basic interests is to protect a good reputation in the eyes of his personal confessor, he will naturally be loathe to divulge any serious sins. The solution to his dilemma is simple, logical, and mathematical: double the number of confessors to accommodate both mortal and venial sins. If this particular subterfuge tends more towards cleverness than rank dishonesty, a second measure, also grounded in a quantitative mode of thinking, casts a darker shadow over the ethical norms traditionally governing the sacrament: in order to dodge the discomfort of having to indict oneself, and yet at the same time go through the requisite motions to obtain absolution, the crafty penitent has only to exploit what is known as a general confession. By charging himself with wholesale sinfulness, he can camouflage particular transgressions in the warp of a multiplicity of sins. If these stratagems maintain a formal compliance with the institutions and articles of the sacrament, they do so to the detriment of its spirit. Lost in the shuffle of quantitative factors bent solely on maintaining surface orderliness are qualitative considerations such as a desire to mend one's ways or a willingness to do penance, considerations that for Pascal would naturally attend the urge to seek forgiveness in the first place.

The lines of opposition on this are drawn especially clear when the Jesuit, in relating his order's precepts on the appropriate consignment of penance, informs Montalte that should the sinner not approve of the penance, he can interrupt the proceedings and, it is implied, shop about for a more accommodating confessor. Or should he opt to atone for his sins later by, in effect, running up a tab in the *hic et nunc* and pay the balance in purgatory, he is to be given a trivial penance so as to maintain "l'intégrité du sacrament." The integrity to which the Jesuit refers is, of course, purely formal and mechanistic. As he is to add a few lines later in response to Montalte's quip that one ought no longer call Confession the sacrament of Penance, "au moins on en donne toujours quelqu'une [une pénitence] *pour la forme.*" Predictably, Pascal's own riposte transforms this categorical question of formal integrity into an indictment of moral fragmentation. His indictment presupposes integrity of a different order, which is none other than the order correlating the absolution of the confessor to the forgiveness of Jesus Christ. "Croyez-vous qu'il soit permis de donner l'absolution indifféremment à tous ceux qui la demande, sans reconnaître auparavant si Jésus Christ délie dans le ciel ceux que vous déliez sur la terre?" (Letter 10, p. 137). The superficial and formalistic bias of the Jesuit conception of the sacrament, as well as the statistical and "democratic " urge underlying that conception, are put into bold relief by the terms of Pascal's objection. Those terms ("indifférément" and "tous ceux qui la demande") defining Jesuit attitude and policy stand in dramatic juxtaposition to the "heart" of the matter, namely a sense on the part of the confessor that the sins have been forgiven by Christ. Pascal wants to underscore here the disjunctive nature of the Jesuit positions. He also wants to remind the Jesuit confessors and their "clients" that these procedures grounded in the logic of the world, a logic that flippantly and erroneously applies arithmetical reasoning, are in their essence a sham. They may seem to ring true; they may even seem to make sense—as long as the discourse of the heart, that is, of the intuitive and the commonsensical, is kept at a distance.[14]

Montalte's barbs are not sufficient to irk the "Jesuit," who is able to reach into his grab bag of maxims and produce a perfectly orthodox position. The casuist Filiutius eloquently maintains the ideal of a coherence of purpose between divine volition and the acts of earthly confessors. Pascal is, however, able to counter this opinion with another passage from this same Filiutius (who had appropriated it from Suarez) that would, in effect, release the confessor from his basic responsibilities. According to the provisions of this maxim, the confessor would be obliged to evaluate the *external* indices of the penitent's resolve or sincerity, but could, even in the face of evidence to the contrary, grant absolution on the basis of an appropriately affirmative answer to the question, "do you abhor sin in your soul?" By juxtaposing the two precepts, Pascal is able to accomplish two things: on the one hand, he reiterates his accusation of rupture in the moral presuppositions governing a proper confession; and on the other, he points to the textual inconsistency of the Jesuit program. And if this last point is important enough to warrant extended examination later on, its practical considerations for the sacrament do not fall outside the focus of these early thoughts on fragmentation. Figuring among these consequences is a special kind of pressure that falls upon the confessor, who finds himself caught between the rock of his own judgment and the hard place of a formal obligation to take the penitent at his word, no matter how hollow that word might ring. This quandry, is, however, only a momentary one in the context of the letter; for should push come to shove and a decision have to be taken, the second course would take precedent. The sinner's word would have to be accepted even if the confessor has reason to suspect immediate recidivism. Montalte is quick to see in all this a devalorization of the confessor's powers of observation. He would be required to believe the contrary of what he sees—and this belief would, like the sacrament itself, end up a sham: "On veut dire [...] qu'ils sont obligés d'agir et d'absoudre comme s'ils croyaient que cette résolution fût ferme et constante, encore qu'ils ne le croient pas en effet." This ends up fragmenting what might be called the moral economy of the confessional insofar as penitents cannot necessarily depend on the "honesty" of confessors who are required to feign belief in the sincerity of other disingenuous penitents' promises of resolve. But if such contamination of the traditional circuit of confidence and sincerity represents for Pascal an assault on the basic premises of the sacrament, even he has to admit that such novelties and aberrations must surely bring on the desired quantitative result by attracting hordes of clients to the Jesuit confessionals (Letter 10, p. 139).

Of course, Pascal deploys the quantitative argument in order to assure that any popular success of the "new" confession, where subterfuges of quantification and fragmentation are valorized, be seen as monstrous. He first suggests that with absolution so easy to obtain, sinners would likely be encouraged to sin. Far from disagreeing, the "Jesuit" seconds the point with a quotation from Bauny. If, for the Jansenists, such attitudes would reduce the sacrament to vapid forms and formulas, to the casuist, Caussin, the alternatives would reduce most sinners to final despair: "Que si elle n'était véritable, l'usage de la confession serait interdit à la plupart du monde; et qu'il n'y aurait plus d'autre remède aux pecheurs, qu'une branche d'arbre et une corde" (Letter 10, p. 139). With this spectacular, fatalistic rationale in place, the Jesuit's answer to Montalte's "induction" that such precepts must draw throngs to Jesuit confessionals comes across as Pascal must have intended it—as bloated and, more importantly, as irrelevant. What Pascal wants his reader to understand is that if the Jesuits are overrun and oppressed by hordes of penitents—"nous sommes accablés et comme opprimés sous la foule de nos pénitents"[15]—one of the main objectives of their order, service to the greatest number of souls, is met. He also wants his reader to understand that this objective is as conceptually defective as the steps taken in its service.

The sense of this defectiveness established in the mind of the reader, Pascal wades more deeply into his adversaries' ethics by numbers. He targets the matter of near occasions of sin, which to the casuistic mind, few sinners really want to avoid. To reconcile this lack of determination with the obligation to avoid such occasions, the casuists have only to reconstitute the notion of "occasion prochaine" by turning to statistical specification similar to the operation performed on the sacrament of Penance. It is not at all a question of the "heart" of the issue, which in this case would be the clear and compelling sense of the danger to which one is exposed. In the new theology, near occasions of sin would be defined as those situations provoking the same sin two or three times a year. So says Escobar. Bauny puts the figure at "once or two times per month"—already a dramatic increase. This in turn is adjusted upwards to "almost daily," which itself evolves into authorization to remain in the precarious situation when to leave it would be cause for public comment. What we see here is Pascal's not so thinly disguised attempt to show that once the frontier of the quantitative has been crossed, and a fragmentational mode of thinking legitimized, any check on increasingly outrageous quantification becomes more and more unlikely.

The outrageousness of this kind of numerologic is underscored later in this same Letter 10, where what would seem to be an exemplary qualitative issue, love of God, is transmuted into an absurd amalgam of opinion on the number of days one is required to love God. The gamut runs from once a year to once every five years, or is limited to specific occasions such as birthdays and holidays. For his part, Montalte finds himself obliged simply to "laisser passer tout ce badinage, où l'esprit de l'homme se joue si insollement de l'amour de Dieu." In so shrugging off the Jesuit's arithmetical tomfoolery, Pascal cuts in several directions. For instance, he locates such activity in "l'esprit de l'homme." He suggests that it is all a matter of a reductive mind game having no rapport with matters of the heart, that is, with the place of faith as well as of intuitive, certain knowledge. Reason, or more exactly, reasoning, infused with contrivance and self-interest, has been given reign in an area falling beyond its jurisdiction. The mind ends up frolicking ("se jouer") in pointless banter ("badinage"), in the playful discourse of something analagous to a parlor game.

In Letter 9, Pascal exposes yet another application, this one almost comical in its baldness, of casuist numerological and fragmentational tactics. Here it is a question of attendance at Mass; or more precisely, of formulas authorizing fractional attendance designed to ensure formal compliance with established obligation. The first maxim trucked out by Montalte's Jesuit dupe is from the "grands théologiens," Hurtado and Convinck. Pascal wants it clear that he is dealing with front-line Jesuit sources, not back-room scribes. These great theologians offer the following opinion: "il suffit d'être présent à la Messe de corps, quoiqu'on soit absent d'esprit, pourvu qu'on demeure dans une contenance respectueuse extérieure." In writing of criteria that simply suffice in fulfilling the duty to attend Mass, these "great theologians" reduce such fulfillment to minimum, mechanical values, to whatever is necessary to tip the balance from noncompliance to technical compliance. This minimum value is corporal presence. It no longer matters—and the point is that it no longer matters *officially*—that the body merely vegetate at Mass while the mind, which in this case, also means the heart, is allowed to wander elsewhere.

   The Mass, the linchpin of the Church's tradition and practice, is to be subordinated to human frailty and caprice; and the only restriction set forth is that a respectful air be maintained in order to guarantee the trappings of piety and to avoid public reaction.[16] This fragmentation of the worshiper, and the public charade required to "legitimize" it, serve as a base from which Pascal can lay into even more basic versions of Jesuit thinking on the matter: "Et Vasquez passe plus avant, car il dit qu'on satisfait au précepte d'ouïr la Messe, encore qu'on ait l'intention de n'en rien faire" (p. 132). The difference between this formulation and the one preceding it is more than slight; for if the earlier maxim might have accommodated human frailty (willing spirit but weak flesh), no importance was laid to intention. There is now, however, a complete break in the circuit between the internal (intention) and the external (satisfaction of a duty). So when Pascal has his Jesuit say that Vasquez "moves further ahead," he is, in fact, saying that the casuist moves further into the secrecy of human motivation. The question then becomes: on what is the original obligation to hear Mass based, and how does this spiritless participation actually fulfill that obligation?

   With the business of intention out on the table, Pascal reaches into the wealth of maxims at his disposal; and as if to show that Vasquez's precept, peculiar though it may be, does not represent the final word on the subject, he turns to the following judgment from Escobar: "Qu'une méchante intention, comme de regarder des femmes avec un désir impur, jointe à celle d'ouïr la messe comme il faut, n'empêche pas qu'on y satisfasse." What in Vasquez had been an absence of appropriate intention is now a dramatic presence of intention which, however inappropriate—in this case a desire to lust after women—may be considered sufficient for satisfaction of the precept when complemented by a simultaneous desire to hear Mass properly. Pascal lets the maxim stand without commentary; or rather, he leaves commentary and analysis to the readers who will have no trouble discerning the bald incompatability of the maxim's clauses, and thus its inappropriateness. He chooses instead to increase his pressure on the casuists by exposing a series of prescriptions whose outrageousness resides in their manifest fragmenting of the Mass to accommodate hurried or disinterested worshipers. In the first of these, the casuists would authorize a simple fractioning of the ritual into two parts with no apparent effect on its unity—unity understood, of course, as a mathematical, not a substantive principle. In this logic, if a + b = c, then b + a must also give c. Consequently, it cannot matter if one first hears the end of the Mass and the beginning afterwards. The second maxim, elaborating on this principle of fractionation, provides for simultaneous attendance at two different Masses. For example, if one Mass is just beginning and the other is at the consecration, one's obligation can be fulfilled all the same "parce qu'on peut avoir l'attention à ces deux côtés à la fois et que deux moitiés de Messe font une Messe entière." With such incontrovertible arithmetic in place, it is a matter of simple extrapolation to justify even more advanced applications. Escobar maintains, for example, that "vous pouvez ouïr la Messe en très peu de temps: si par exemple, vous rencontrez quatre Messes à la fois, qui soient tellement assorties, que quand l'une commence, l'autre soit à l'Evangile, une autre à la Consecration et la dernière à la Communion." By way of response, Montalte merely pursues the logic of the progression and suggests that given the number of chapels at Notre-Dame, one could very well hear an entire Mass there in the wink of an eye.

This fragmentational view of the Mass would also hold advantages for the celebrant, who by following the casuist logic, could increase his profit by parceling the Mass into transferable entities. On this point and on those to follow, namely simony, almsgiving, and the determination of the monetary value of human life itself, it is clear that the casuist numerologic assumes broader jurisdiction and that it stands as a fundamental feature of the morality Pascal qualifies as modern, aberrant, and pernicious. Moreover, the moral practices deriving from investment in the quantitative are simply the most manifest and natural consequences of a fundamental substitution of reason for faith, and of rationalization for the claims of the heart. Now, in terms of payments to priests, Pascal does not question the basic premise. He will in fact specify that "l'Eglise permet aux prêtres qui sont pauvres de recevoir de l'argent pour leurs messes, parce qu'il est bien juste que ceux qui servent à l'autel vivent de l'autel. . . ." His argument targets the divisive and fragmentational effect the ethic of exchange, once it has been given the status of a basic operating procedure, can have on the integrity of the Mass and its celebrant. In these maxims, the Mass comes across as a mathematical, commercial variable, a kind of currency. As such, it can be broken down into pieces to permit the celebrant to maximize his profits by selling off parcels. The affiliated principles of divisibility and marketability would then give the casuist a conceptual precedent, as they would give Pascal a rhetorical springboard into codes of behavior in which supposed responsibility toward the paying customer would be privileged over responsibility toward the institution:

> Les prêtres qui ont reçu de l'argent pour dire la messe tous les jours la doivent dire tous les jours et qu'ils ne peuvent pas s'excuser sur ce qu'ils ne sont pas toujours assez bien préparés pour la dire, parce qu'on peut toujours faire l'acte de contrition; et que s'ils y manquent, c'est leur faute et non pas celle de celui qui leur fait dire la messe.

There would be no excuse based on morality—"ils ne peuvent pas s'excuser"—potent enough to abrogate the contract based on the exchange of money for service. The qualitative issue of proper spiritual preparation takes an evident back seat to the concept of duty based, in theory, on the principle of respect of the contract; in practice, on the more terrestrial principle of monetary advancement.

Parrying the fragmentational assaults on the Mass, Pascal has Montalte argue the point that the Mass is "une chose si grande et si sainte." He wants to underscore in an implicit but clear way its unicity. Indeed, what is most forceful about this element of his riposte is its very simplicity. The grandeur and sanctity of the Mass as conceived in tradition are so evident that further rhetorical support at this point would be superfluous. He then adds that those same two qualities serve as guarantors, as unmoving points of reference with an inherent capacity to confound and refute the postulations of the casuists: "Car la Messe est une chose si grande et si sainte, qu'il suffirait, pour faire perdre à vos auteurs toute créance dans l'esprit de plusieurs personnes, de leur montrer de quelle manière ils en parlent."

Of the "manners in which the casuists speak" of the Mass, some come across even more strongly than these rather comical examples of arithmetical fragmentation. In order to suggest that numerologic, once in place, tends naturally to degenerate into, and generate, more and more outrageous positions, Pascal publicizes in Letter 6 the following thought:

La pluralité des messes apporte tant de gloire à Dieu, et tant d'utilité aux âmes, que j'oserais dire, avec notre Père Cellot, dans son livre de la Hiérarchie, p. 611 de l'impression de Rouen, qu'il n'y aurait pas trop de prêtres, quand non seulement tous les hommes et les femmes, si cela se pouvait, mais que les corps insensibles, et les bêtes brutes même, *bruta animalia,* seraient changés en prêtres pour célébrer la messe.

Left behind in the rubble of the "logic" transforming the inherent value of the Mass into a rationale for easing restriction of priests' worthiness to celebrate the rite, is all sense of the qualitative. Under Pascal's pen and editing, this reasoning, emblematic of the numerological politic of serving the greatest number of souls and of having maxims in place for all moral predicaments and social classes, literally ends up brutalizing the sanctity of the Mass. The casuists are shown to be unable or unwilling to distinguish between categories: quality and quantity are interchangeable; animals and inanimate objects can, in the wildness of this thinking, be considered, if only rhetorically, potential candidates for the priesthood; priests equal Masses; more priests equal more Masses; and more Masses equal more glory for God and more utility for needy souls.

On a certain level, the argument may not be without its allure. It is, however, contaminated locally by the outlandishness of its extension into the wild kingdom. On a more general level, the argument in favor of more priests and Masses loses the validity it might otherwise have had by the larger context in which it is situated—and in which Pascal makes sure it is perceived as being situated. That context of modifications and modernizations would include a number of maxims rationalizing corrupt financial dealings within the Church. The most prominent of these are the ones providing technical detours around simony. Pascal wants his readers to see how deeply into the Church's infrastructure, teachings, and tradition casuist quantification can cut. Among the practices the Jansenists found to be most galling were those that tended to turn the Church into a commercial operation where services and offices were bought and sold as any marketplace commodity. The justification of simony, for example, would be a logical extension of a kind of thinking in which quantity is given qualitative status, insofar as it is considered by the casuists as a valid position from which to argue, or with which to justify certain practices.

For Pascal's casuist, the issue is basic and simple: if traditional Thomistic definitions continue to be honored, the old brand of simony would run rampant in the modern church. The way to counter the "scandal" of strict adherence to the traditional sense of simony is, it appears, to engage in a kind of shell game in which the money changing hands would itself be changed into something less tangible and thus less imputable. The casuist Valentia—with some editorial prompting from Pascal—puts it this way:

> Si l'on donne un bien temporel pour un bien spirituel, c'est-à-dire de l'argent pour un bénéfice [Pascal interrupts here to ground the terms in the concrete], et qu'on donne l'argent comme le prix du bénéfice, c'est une simonie visible; mais si on le donne comme le motif qui porte la volonté du collateur à le conférer, ce n'est point simonie, encore que celui qui le confère, considère et attende l'argent comme la fin principale. (Letter 6, p. 89)

The exchange of money as remuneration for the "bénéfice" would thus be fully identifiable with simony as normally understood; it would be "visible." The trick is to hide the offending concept, *price,* under an appropriate shell so that it no longer produces "visible" simony. In the casuistic shuffling of terms, causes, and effects, that shell would be something of a marketing campaign designed to deflect the crass economic resonances of the operation. This would be managed by spiriting the whole thing away into the far less visible realm of the psychological.[17] Price is transformed into motivation, a move that would be potent enough not only to reduce the visibility of the simony, but to expunge it completely ("il n'y a point de simonie"). This total disappearance under the shell of motivation is all the more mysterious in that the person conferring the *bien spirituel* is in no way obliged to pretend that the money itself has disappeared, or has been sublimated. Indeed the *collateur* is permitted to "consider and look to the money as the principal end" of the affair. By this sort of mental legerdemain, the casuists would have nipped "une infinité de simonies" in the bud.

Finally, the new guidelines for simony would be based on a peculiar view of charity. As Pascal's Jesuit voice asks: "qui serait assez méchant pour refuser, en donnant de l'argent pour un bénéfice, de porter son intention à le donner comme *un motif* qui porte le bénéficier à le résigner, au lieu de le donner comme *le prix* du bénéfice?" (Letter 6, p. 89). That Pascal puts both "motif" and "prix" in italics serves to highlight the precise equivalence he wants his readers to see in these terms, an equivalence eloquently denouncing the sham of the maxim. The point is driven home in the final words of the paragraph: when Montalte declares that everyone has the "grâces suffisantes" to cut such a deal ("faire un tel marché"), he conjoins the present proceedings back to Letter 2 in which the controversial term "grâce suffisante" had been effectively exposed as nonsensical and, incidentally, as running counter to Thomistic thinking; which is also the explicit case in the deliberations on simony. Pascal has his Jesuit admit that "Saint Thomas y est contraire, en ce qu'il enseigne que c'est toujours simonie de donner un bien spirituel pour un temporel, si le temporel en est la fin" (p. 89).

An equally "sufficient grace" is put at the disposition of those who balk at the thought of having to part with a portion of their wealth. In their reworking of the scriptural obligation to donate the *superflu* of one's goods, the casuists arrange the terms so that this *superflu* remains just out of reach; or more precisely, that it remains always within the margins of the necessary. A maxim by "le docte Vasquez" would be sufficient to legitimize the point:

> Ce que les personnes du monde gardent pour relever leur condition et celle de leur parents n'est pas appelé superflu; et c'est pourquoi à peine trouver-t-on qu'il y ait jamais de superflu dans les gens du monde, et non pas même dans les rois. (Letter 6, p. 85)

In this view, ordinary language is refashioned to serve an ethic of unchecked growth. Indeed, the system as expressed would be completely open-ended. The maxim is predicated on that which is retained to advance ("relever") personal or familial fortune. So the maxim effectively works both sides of the issue: on the one hand, the qualitative, by establishing a perceptible, formally affirmative response to the question of whether or not the rich are required to give as alms their superfluous wealth; and on the other, the quantitative, by redefining, for the benefit of those whose ambition and life-style demand an ever-increasing accumulation of material goods, the very notion of what the term superfluous means.

If, in this instance, Pascal spotlights a mode of thinking that opens up onto an undefined, ungraspable quantity; in Letter 7 he will show the other side of the coin, the casuists' scandalous quantification of nothing less than life itself, which would stand as the ultimate valorization of the procedure for displacing moral responsibility and imputability. That procedure, the direction of intention, is touted as the "principe merveilleux" and the "grande méthode" of Jesuitical casuistry. Before turning him loose

with the appropriately shocking maxims, Pascal first has his Jesuit explain
the principle of this marvelous method. We then learn that it is a matter of
providing psychological detours around manifestly offensive notions. In so
doing, the letter of laws proscribing such practices can be maintained,
thereby allowing for mutations of their spirit. This allows the casuist
theoretician to step with impunity into the fascinating and unbounded
domain of individual circumstance. On the matter of vengeance, for
example, the casuist voice will show precisely how the direction of intention
is able to realize an unholy alliance between the scriptural maxims and those
of the world. As point of departure, the casuist text quotes first the New
Testament and then Hebrew scriptures. In both laws, vengeance would be
manifestly forbidden. To seek vengeance would be to exchange evil for evil
and would "attirer sur soi la vengeance de Dieu." The casuist would then
take this notion of the "equal" exchange of evil and distill it to render a kind
of mathematical objectivity: since the two evils are in an equational
relationship, it stands to reason that, if we can substitute for one of the
equivalent terms something as clearly desirable as the evil is reprehensible,
the equation will come apart. The balance will be tipped and a laundered
version of vengeance can be pursued in good conscience. In this case, that
something is the conservation of honor. To conserve one's honor is, of
course, an honorable intention. Indeed it is the stuff of great tragi-
comedies: it defines heroism.[18]

With the "heroic" principle of saving one's honor in place, a second,
more explicit, version of the maxim can be deployed. In this formulation,
culled from Lessius, the high sounding, but rather abstract and elusive
notion of honor is focused on a specific act, a slap: "Celui qui a reçu un
soufflet ne peut pas avoir l'intention de s'en venger; mais il peut bien avoir
celle d'eviter l'infamie, et pour cela de repousser à l'instant cette injure, et
même à coups d'épée." And if the provocation has been specified, the
response, being part of the original equationary thinking, can now also be
specified: conserving honor has therefore been modified into "coups
d'épée." That the maxim allows for an instantaneous response to the
offense against personal honor ("repousser à l'instant cette injure") would,
in effect, further legitimize a code of conduct predicated on what had
previously been described as the logic of the world; that is, the logic of
amour-propre, willfulness and appetite. After several intervening maxims
in which this concrete example is supported by more abstract and thus less
shocking formulations—for example, wishing for or praying to God for the

adversary's death—Pascal has his Jesuit resituate the issue in the context of worldly imperatives. One of the most pressing of those imperatives is, of course, money; and in this case, the prospect for material gain would justify a son's longing for, and rejoicing over, the death of his father, provided that the desire and glee are motivated by "le bien qui lui revient, et non pas par une haine personnelle."

Scandalous though it may be, such psychological violence is but an intermediate station along the way of Pascal's romp through the maxims on homicide. For just as his debunking in the early letters of nonsensical expressions such as *pouvoir prochain* and *grâce suffisante* had relied on real-world, ordinary language models, Pascal will want to expose real-world applications of these psychological precedents. To this end he baits his host—in fact he dares him—to provide thinking to justify duels. Now this subject is an especially inviting one given the ongoing, if not always successful, campaign by Church and State against the practice. The Jesuit is prompt in giving satisfaction: a casuist maxim allows the challenged party to show up at the designated place, not to duel, but to defend himself should his adversary, who might think him a chicken (the term appears in the maxim), also show up and press the attack. But Pascal wants more than this sort of deflective or circumlocutional authorization of dueling. He wants to thrust directly into the meat of the matter; so he unsheaths a maxim that would permit dueling "en mots propres, pourvu qu'on dirige son intention à l'accepter seulement pour conserver son honneur ou sa fortune." This thought, adapted from the thinking of the casuist Layman, would then complement the notion of conservation of honor, which had governed the majority of the previous maxims, with a more material consideration, the welfare of one's fortune. This move into the material world is to become more explicit in the next selection which, to the obvious advantage of the system Pascal seems to be putting in place, would give sole billing to the exigencies of purse and property: "Qu'on peut se battre en duel pour défendre même son bien, s'il n'y a que ce moyen de le conserver; parce que chacun a le droit de défendre son bien et même par la mort de ses ennemis" (Letter 7, p. 100).

One should not forget, however, that up to this point the whole subject has been treated from the perspective of one who has to react to the challenge of an aggressor. Pascal next orients the issue to show that it is altogether possible to propose the duel. The text he chooses comes from Sanchez's *Théologie morale* and, in legitimizing the challenge ("il est permis d'accepter et d'offrir le duel"), also specifies that the goods one can legitimately protect by dueling be "en quantité considérable." And if at first look this seems to extend the quantitative factor beyond the realm of common usage, one has only to remember how the term "superflu" had been distorted to the advantage of reluctant almsgivers. More importantly, this initial instance of specification would set the stage for an even more dramatic flurry of "pricing." Indeed, Montalte will broach the subject directly: "Mais, mon Père, après avoir si bien pourvu à l'honneur, n'avez-vous rien fait pour le bien? Je sais qu'il est de moindre considération, mais il n'importe. Il me semble qu'on peut bien diriger son intention à tuer pour le conserver" (Letter 7, p. 105). The response he gets is, of course, exactly what the Jansenist ordered. In effect, it would permit the killing of some-one who has violated the sanctity of private property even when the menace of personal danger has passed. Moreover, in the passage that follows, the reader is treated to a spectacular devalorization of human life.

The matter is first cast into characteristically general terms: the casuist, in direct response to Montalte's request for precision regarding the minimum value of property and the right to kill in its defense, declares that the thing must be of "great value in the judgment of a prudent man." Montalte is quick to point out the obvious inconvenience of this formulation: in this world peopled in large part with imprudent souls, the odds of finding a reliable assessor, "un homme prudent" could hardly be called favorable. Indeed, the casuist is "inclined," if only momentarily, and if only to prepare a stronger case for Pascal, to agree, exclaiming that it is no small matter to compare the life of a man, of a Christian man at that, to money. The difficulty of assigning precise value to such an elusive commodity—it should be recalled that there has been a transference whereby the object of value, the property, at first standing in for the life of the offender, has in fact been replaced by that life itself—is as eloquent an argument as could be found for the need for casuist enlightenment: "C'est ici où je veux vous faire sentir la nécessité de nos casuistes." At the base of this most pressing necessity is the unfavorable precedent of scripture which on the subject of killing provides no elaboration, no special case scenarios, and certainly no consideration of market value. To the casuist, the unadorned pro-scription, "vous ne tuerez point," is but the hollow echoing of voices no longer in step with the complexity of contemporary morality. It falls then to the new casuists to dare determine the proper sums and values. This term "oser" cuts two ways: within the internal, manipulative discourse

(Montalte/"Jesuit"), *oser* might be read as the semantic equivalent of "have the courage" (to reform old-fashioned and simplistic thinking that is out of step with modern exigencies). In terms of the discourse in which Pascal engages real-life Jesuits, the verb carries a clearly negative charge: how could the casuists even think of such a thing?

In the next sentence, Pascal sets up a less than subtle—and thereby wholly appropriate—rhetorical imbalance. On the one hand, and in counterpoint to "tous les anciens pères" who have been exiled as ancient history, stands Molina. He is featured as "great, incomparable, the glory of the Jesuits and as possessing inimitable prudence." In short, he would be the very one to fit the requisites established by Tannerus and Reginaldus, that the one to determine the value of human life be "un homme prudent." On the other hand, and coming fast on the heels of this frantic myth-making, are the six or seven ducats at which Molina, exercising inimitable prudence, affixes the value of human life. The inverse function Pascal wants to establish between Molina's reknown and a quantitative devalorization of human life is to beome even more spectacular. From Molina's quill comes yet another devaluation: this man of inimitable prudence "would not dare impute any sin at all to he who kills a person with designs on property valued at one *écu*—or less" (Letter 7, p. 105). So the six or seven ducats can fall to one *écu*. By the same token, Molina has given ample testimony of his prudence by reserving judgment, that is, by not daring to intervene. The second, perhaps more disturbing, formulation comes as a general rule of conduct established by Escobar. In this precept, Molina's prudent refusal to pass judgment now strongly resembles a formula, an arithmetical truth in which, significantly, Molina has been enshrined as an irrefutable voice of authority: "régulièrement on peut tuer un homme pour la valeur d'un écu, selon Molina" (Letter 14, p. 191). The devaluation will continue until it seems that one is permitted to kill for something as trivial as an apple, if its loss would impune one's honor and reputation (Letter 14, p. 193).

The trajectory Pascal traces here may be taken as paradigmatic of the course that investment in the logic of numbers—which is the logic of rationalization, and the language of the "ville de trouble"[19]—is bound inevitably to follow. Faith in this fragmentational mode of thinking leads quickly to fragmentation of entities—for example, the Mass, one's love of God, and human life itself—that tradition and common sense define as whole. Pascal wants to show that casuistical fragmentation is, at best, silly or scandalous. At worst, as in the case of homicide, it is a threat to the order of things and can lead to chaos. The social and political chaos, in the form of dueling and homicide, is the manifest version of the moral chaos that issues, in part at least, from the substitution of the number for the Word. As we shall now see, among the traditions trammelled by casuist logicality are certain assumptions and conventions basic to language itself.

Chapter 2

Magic Words and Powerful Speech Acts: Casuist Abuse of Language in the *Provinciales*

THE FRAGMENTATIONAL THINKING in which Pascal wants to implicate his adversaries will touch not only on the way they use language, but also on certain presuppositions and conventions of language itself. Indeed, of the tasks facing him straightaway as public relations manager of Port-Royal's campaign to cut its political and ideological losses—the censure of Arnauld being a foregone conclusion, it could hardly be a question of saving his seat at the Sorbonne—there is one that seems to have struck Pascal as especially urgent: to curry public support for Jansenist positions by factoring a heated and heady theological dispute into more accessible categories and language. The general lines of this factoring can be seen in the delimitation of the "question of fact" which concerns Arnauld's skill as reader of the *Augustinus*. "La question sur cela est de savoir s'il a pu, sans témérité, témoigner par là qu'il doute que ces propositions soient de Jansénius, après que Messieurs les évêques ont déclaré qu'elles y sont" (Letter 1, p. 35). On the one hand, the argument of experience, evidence, and interpretation (be it controversial or not); on the other, the argument of force, intractability, and declaration. And even if Montalte quickly dismisses this factual question as "peu importante," the issue of authority that it raises will cut across virtually all the *Lettres*. In this case, the question is whether strong words—a declaration on the part of the bishops—is to prevail over the arguments of common sense and due process. In a broader perspective, the question is whether the strong words of revealed truth and Church tradition are to prevail over the "arguments" of desire and self-interest.

Now, since at this stage of the proceedings, the allegations against Arnauld seem to revolve around the doctrinal legitimacy of his belief that grace was withheld from Saint Peter when he denied any association with Christ, Pascal will allow his fictional voice, Montalte, to assume that at the heart of the dispute lie the important issues of efficacious grace, its forcefulness, and its apportionment. He then goes about the business of "discovering" before his readers' eyes that efficacious grace itself is not the point, and that the dispute over it is, in fact, an elemental component of a conspiracy against the person of Arnauld as much as it is against the theological case he pleads. More precisely, Montalte discovers that this conspiracy is built around certain linguistic presuppositions whose anomalous character he will be only too disposed to publicize. In this regard he will manipulate his readers by presenting them with the argument that terms such as "proximate power" and "sufficient grace," which, in the discourse of the anti-Jansenist forces, would carry theological significance, are at bottom a linguistic hoop through which the Jansenists are being forced to jump. "En quel termes sommes-nous réduits?" is the question a bemused and irritated Montalte will have to ask in Letter 2. It is then essential to Pascal's strategy of defense that the events of 1655 be perceived as a war of words in which logic, common sense, and linguistic convention—not doctrine *per se*—are at stake.

In the first three letters he confects a relentless exposé of Molinist violence to linguistic convention. This violence would operate on the basic level of the sign itself, fragmenting it into private and forceful devices of oppression. By exposing this attack on the foundations of language, the writer of the letters can hope to undermine in a general way the conventionality and credibility of the Jesuits' word and teaching. The most conspicuous form of violence to language centers on what, for the sake of discussion, might be called the magic word. Unlike ordinary language, grounded in public agreement on the rapport of representation between words and things, between signifier and signified, magic language, referring back to its own articulation rather than to any external referent, is, by design, obscure and obscurantist. Magic language also presumes as one of its basic functions a political discrimination between the initiated and those for whom the language holds no meaning other than the force by which it excludes them from the happy few.

Of course, Pascal does not just come out and accuse his adversaries of twisting language to their own ends. His approach is more clever, more playful, and, as a result, more effective. It allows him to make what in a later letter he will call "une entrée insensible en matière." This entrance will move him to set up a series of rhetorical strawmen, the first of which concerns all the goings on at the Sorbonne. Now, in light of its fractious and chronic nature, this activity would, to any thinking person, have to bear significantly on either doctrine or practice. As far as the *question de fait* is concerned, Pascal/Montalte exposes certain irregularities in the deliberations at the Sorbonne; namely the fundamental irrelevance of allegations of temerity against Arnauld and the curious refusal of the anti-Jansenists to provide textual evidence of the five propositions. As for the *question de droit,* he can claim to have recently and easily become a working theologian. He has taken the bull by the horns by seeking the wisdom of supposed experts. The first witness is M.N., model of anti-Jansenist zeal. Indeed, M.N.'s zeal is said to be matched only by Montalte's own ardent curiosity, which had recently been piqued by the uproar over the conclusions Arnauld draws in his interpretation of Saint Peter's fall. The conclusions would be these: grace is not given to all men, but when given, it is unfailing in its effect on the will; it is, in short, efficacious.[1] These two points would, it seems, be at the heart of the difference between the two camps. Montalte is to find, however, that all is not what it seems, and that there is less here than meets the eye. In his first encounter with M.N., he discovers that not only do the Jansenists' adversaries *not* concur among themselves on what would seem to derive logically from their divergence with Arnauld; that grace is accorded to all men; but, more to the point, that such a conclusion, for all its logic, is not even the point: "il me rebuta rudement et me dit que ce n'était pas là le point." To the informed reader or to the reader being informed by the supposed discoveries of Montalte, the theological *differend* between Jansenist and Molinist could not then be part of the debate on the apportionment of grace. This conclusion is corroborated by M.N.'s remarkably convenient adherence in public to an even more appropriate passage from Saint Augustine, announcing literally that "la grâce n'est pas donnée à tous." On the second point—whether or not this grace not given to all men does, when given, determine the will to take correct action— Montalte discovers that he was no less "confused" than on the first point. Indeed, the rudeness of M.N.'s rebuttal on the first point is complemented by Montalte's ill luck on the second ("je ne fus pas plus heureux en cette seconde question"). He has, to all appearances, wholly misunder-stood the anti-Jansenist theology, since, in the words of the zealous adversary, the unfailing efficacy of this grace would be fully consistent with orthodox theology.

With the purely theological objections to Arnauld's position thus disarmed, Montalte, in order to come out of the darkness, and in order to enlighten his provincial reader, will have to take the more frontal approach of begging his interlocutor to specify just what then might be the nature of Arnauld's heresy. The answer he gets serves to plunge the issue into a purely sectarian bath: "c'est qu'il ne reconnaît pas que les justes aient le pouvoir d'accomplir les commandements de Dieu *en la manière que nous l'entendons*" (Letter 1, p. 37). At last Montalte is in touch with what he terms the "nœud" of the affair—the knot being not only the essential point, the principal dilemma as in a stage play, and the thing to be untied or explained, but also part of the device with which to entangle, constrain, and, in the end perhaps, help to hang his adversaries. He then contacts a Jansenist who is as adamant in his support of Augustinian theology as M.N. is opposed to it. "Feigning" allegiance to the party of his host—which, since he does in fact bear such allegiance, would be a double feint—he refocuses the issue by asking if the Sorbonne could conceivably introduce the doctrinal error that the just always have the power to obey God's law. His reason for broaching the issue from this particular angle is more blatant than in the previous cases: "pour en être mieux reçu, je feignis d'être fort des siens." In other words, he lets his reader know that he understands from the outset that the idea of the just always being able to obey the commandments is basic to the Jansenist position. The advantage of such a gambit is fairly clear in the response he elicits from his Jansenist; namely, that this supposed error is so obviously Catholic that only Lutheran and Calvinist heretics could think otherwise; and that he, as a Jansenist, and thus as an orthodox Catholic, holds as anathema and heretical the positions of Protestant dissidents.

Montalte, pleading surprise in the face of this "unexpected" answer, suggests that he may have overplayed his Jansenist sympathies. Since Jansenist theology has already been associated with Protestantism, that is, with heresy, his surprise must come from the violence of the distinction his interviewee seems to want to make with those other sects. This surprise moves Montalte to ask his interlocutor to "dire confidemment" his view on the issue. Now this adverb serves the Jansenist position in two ways: on the one hand, it can mean "with confidence" (this would be the primary sense of the term as used in Pascal's sentence); on the other, it can mean "in confidence." Taken together, the two senses point to a posture of sincerity and conviction: the Jansenist's position would be viable and consistent both on a personal (confidential) and on the public level, one in which one can have confidence. Moreover, in "s'échauffant" at Montalte's reiteration of the matter, the Jansenist, seconding the Molinists' zeal ("d'un zèle dévot"), proclaims that the point under consideration is an essential aspect of Augustinian and Thomistic theology.

In appealing to these authoritative voices, Pascal is able to establish a link with the Molinist position of several paragraphs earlier, where both Augustine and "tous les thomistes" are cited as guarantors of that position. The point of this synthesis operating under the twin aegis of Augustine and Aquinas is to give a happy Montalte—he is portrayed as "bien satisfait"—a fine reason to return to his zealous Molinist and trumpet the good news of a reconciliation between the two camps. On the point of the capacity of the just to obey the commandments, there seems to be clear agreement. Indeed, the Jansenist adherence to this point as just expressed by M.N.'s brother-in-law, "Jansenist if ever there was one," is so credible that Montalte can certify that the Jansenists would be apt to die in its defense ("j'en étais garant [...] je le leur ferais signer de leur sang"). It is at this point, where adherence to the concept of efficacious grace touches up against suggestions of heroism and martyrdom, that the Molinist brings it all to a quick fade with his "tout beau." It appears that to see "la fin" one has necessarily to be a theologian—a stipulation which in linking theological expertise, finesse, and conclusiveness on this one issue performs two important functions in Pascal's discourse. First, it suggests that the questions being debated and batted about are not theological issues, but rather, theologians' issues; and secondly, it will underscore, and thus further ironize, Montalte's claim of having lately and quickly become a great theologian. What the reader is to discover is that ascent to this rank of "great theologian" does not necessarily mean that one can manage with confidence the issues at hand; for the difference between the positions confronting the various parties to the debate, which is at bottom the difference between orthodoxy and heresy, is "si subtile" (as fine as *le fin* and as conclusive as *la fin*) that the very ones who maintain, advertise, and exploit that difference have themselves no easy time grasping it. This difficulty arises from the fact—and the fact is fine—that even if the Jansenists agree with the Molinists that the just always have the power to obey God's precepts, they do not properly modify this power with the adjective *proximate*. "Contentez-vous donc de savoir que les Jansénistes vous diront bien que tous les justes ont toujours le pouvoir d'accomplir les commandements: "ce n'est pas de quoi nous disputons; mais il ne vous diront pas que ce pouvoir soit *prochain;* c'est là le point" (Letter 1, p. 38). The dispute boils down to—it boils over this one word— a word that is characterized as "le point." This point would then be the fulcrum upon which the difference between inclusion and banishment is gauged and displayed. The point is also the head of the ideological and linguistic weapon turned against the Jansenists, the weapon Pascal will effectively turn back against the Molinist aggressors. Indeed, this word/point, "nouveau et inconnu," would, in the fiction Pascal puts to the service of his cause, have an immediate and violent consequence. It would prick the illusion of understanding ("Jusque-là j'avais entendu les affaires") and send Montalte hurtling into the darkness of ignorance ("ce terme me jeta dans l'obscurité"). What is more, this *prochain* is said to be couched in mystery ("il [the Molinist] m'en fit un mystère") and, as such, would by definition fall beyond the limits of common understanding and be accessible only to the initiated; and the initiated, if we can generalize from the Molinist's response, are not at all disposed to let the uninitiated in on the secret. Indeed, Pascal wants it understood clearly that the language of the Molinists and the positions based on it are by design both fragmented and fragmentational.[2]

This term, qualified earlier as the one the Jansenists will not say, would now be so mysterious, so far removed from either traditional theological discourse or ordinary language, that Montalte, off to consult the Jansenists, finds himself obliged to charge his memory with it, as his intelligence is of no use in retaining it. Indeed, he must make haste to get to his Jansenist's place lest he forget this bizarre word. Once arrived, he quickly pops the question of whether or not his host "admits" this term *prochain.* Asked in his turn to be more precise, Montalte must once again confess that he is blocked on the level of understanding: "Comme ma connaissance n'allait pas jusque-là, je me vis en terme de [ne] lui pouvoir répondre." This response would define a state (*terme*) of intellectual impotence issuing from a single *terme*; and it is surely not without playful malice that Pascal intones the other element of the controversial expression, *pouvoir,* in this admission of impotence; for just as the term *prochain* had been singled out earlier as the only difference between Molinist and Jansenist understanding of this power to keep the commandments, the term "pouvoir" is, in this admission, a completely viable and usable element of language, while *prochain,* the mysterious, meaningless, and "unspeakable" word is hidden off behind the generic element *terme.* Insisting on clarification, Montalte is to find out that if the Molinists themselves are divided on the meaning of the expression *pouvoir prochain,* they stand united on its functional value, which is to present a common, numerically superior front with which to bring down the great Arnauld.

> Vous êtes bien peu instruit. Ils sont si peu dans les mêmes sentiments, qu'ils en ont de tout contraires. Mais, étant tous unis dans le dessein de perdre M. Arnauld, ils se sont avisés de s'accorder de ce terme de *prochain,* que les uns et les autres diraient ensemble, quoiqu'ils l'entendissent diversement, afin de parler un même langage, et que, par cette conformité apparante, ils pussent former un corps considérable, et composer le plus grand nombre, pour l'opprimer avec assurance. (Letter 1, p. 39)

Pascal wants his readers to make the evident inference that the politics of quantification generate policies of language whose sole purpose is to advance an action that only seems to be theological.

The polarity set up in this analysis between *entendre diversement* and *dire ensemble* is to be the dominant point of discussion for the remainder of the letter. Montalte's astonishment at what he has just heard moves him to put aside for the time being his consideration of the unsavory political designs of the Molinists. He can thus imply that as unsavory and as unjustified as those designs may be, they pale in comparison to the illogic and boldness of the means confected to realize them. Of interest to him is this diversity of meaning that Arnauld's adversaries would give to the expression *pouvoir prochain,* qualified once again as the "mot mystérieux." Following a series of encounters—first, with the disciple of M. Le Moyne (professor of theology at the Sorbonne and main anti-Jansenist spokesman); secondly, with the followers of Père Nicolai (the Dominicans) and, finally, with the two groups assembled together—Montalte will relentlessly highlight the Molinists' phonological investment in *pouvoir prochain.* For example, having shown the Jacobins to be in fundamental disagreement with the disciples of Le Moyne over the necessity of efficacious grace (the latter maintaining that this form of divine intervention is superfluous to *pouvoir prochain;* the former taking a position consonant with the Jansenist or Augustinian view, which maintains that it is heresy to deny the need for this efficacious grace), Montalte sees himself justified in realigning the principal participants in the dispute. The Jansenists would be Catholic and allied with the Dominicans; Le Moyne and his disciples heretical. The Jacobin is forced to agree with the logical consequences of Montalte's investigation. His "oui," seemingly firm in its simplicity, apparently needing no further comment, is nonetheless followed fast by "mais." Assent yields to a shift in thinking that does violence to the logic and appropriateness of the assent. The mélange of "yes" (we are in agreement with the Jansenists on the principle of the thing) and "no" (we are, rather, in agreement with M. Le Moyne in naming the power "proximate," which is to say we are not in agreement with the Jansenists at all) finds an analogue in the next paragraph. Montalte, at first maintaining astonishment at the fortuitous appearance of Le Moyne's disciple, tells us that the Jacobins and the disciples of Le Moyne are in fact "continuellement *mêlés* les uns avec les autres," an observation designed to suggest both political colusion and conceptual confusion.

It is not, then, without interest that Le Moyne's disciple arrives just in the nick of time to take the heat off his Dominican allies who, when faced with the pressing logic of Montalte's inference that they are simply playing with words, "ne répondent rien." Montalte has in effect reduced them to a silence connoting either an unshakeable stubbornness or the paralysis of checkmate. That they are referred to as *"mes* Pères"—the use of the possessive pronoun will be fairly constant across the *Provinciales*— underscores the latter: Montalte has his adversaries where he wants them. He then turns to the disciple of Le Moyne and proposes to him the case of a personal acquaintance who holds to the notion that the just always have the power to pray to God but that they still need a shot of efficacious grace to move them to this prayer. In response to Montalte's question as to whether or not the acquaintance, who, incidentally, bears an uncanny ideological resemblance both to Antoine Arnauld *and* to the Dominican fathers seated before him, would be considered heretical, Le Moyne's disciple, who apparently wants neither to be taken by surprise nor to be lead too deeply into the intricacies of substantive issues, insists on slowing things down. The critical point—and Pascal has his character slow things down in order to cue the reader as to this importance—is to dislocate the theoretical issue of grace, transforming this gauge of orthodoxy into a purely linguistic or phonological instrument. This transformation is to take the form of an unflappable investment in the enunciation of the mysterious expression: "s'il appelle ce pouvoir *pouvoir prochain,* il sera thomiste, et partant catholique; sinon il sera janséniste, et partant hérétique." The *distinguo* with which Le Moyne's disciple launches his analysis of the issue functions then not only as a dash of schoolishness thrown in for comic measure by Pascal, it also announces the drawing of ideological lines via a clear and careful distinction ("allons doucement") between Thomistic Catholics on the one hand and Jansenist "heretics" on the other.

Pascal will have his reader understand this investment as radically and exclusively phonological. It is not, as one might expect, a matter of alignment with the principle of the thing, with the announcers of *pouvoir prochain* or even with some alternative (nonorthodox) camp which uses another term to designate this power. The determining issue is physical articulation. Nothing less than public adherence—actual voicing of the expression—is to be accepted as an index of orthodoxy. *Pouvoir prochain* has thus been defined as an ideological password. "Il ne l'appelle ni prochain, ni non-prochain. Il est donc hérétique" (Letter 1, p. 41). It is important to note here that the noncompliance Pascal speaks of cannot yet be understood as noncompliance with a *concept*. Once again, the conceptual elements of the debate—and of Montalte's investigation—have been put aside in order to give full consideration to phonological eccentricities. This is made even clearer in the next exchange where Montalte justifies the noncompliance of his acquaintance by underscoring the refusal of the term's exponents to define just what is meant by *pouvoir prochain*. At this point, one of the Jacobins   who with the rest of the Dominican cohort had just nodded mute, doltish assent to the conclusions expressed by Le Moyne's disciple—makes a movement towards providing such definition by bringing substance back into the discussion and thus breaking clear, if only momentarily, from the more dominant voice of the Sorbonne. He is cut off instantly by that voice and is asked accusingly if he intends to reignite the conceptual skirmishing between the allies: "Voulez-vous recommencer nos brouilleries?" The plural would seem to suggest here that these differences have been ongoing, heated, and bitter. Le Moyne's disciple then goes on to put the Dominican in his place by reminding him of the deal they had struck in common to use this uncommon terminology: "ne sommes-nous pas demeurés d'accord de ne point expliquer ce terme de *prochain* et de le dire de part et d'autre sans dire ce qu'il signifie?" (Letter 1, p. 41).

Pascal has clearly upped the ante. What had been coming across on one level as a somewhat tentative, even confused, understanding between the anti-Arnauld forces at the Sorbonne and the Dominicans is now given a manifestly conspiratorial patina. If, a few paragraphs earlier, the Dominican had denied any affiliation with the Jansenists because of his order's agreement with M. Le Moyne, the notion of agreement here takes on a considerably more muscular aspect. This is due in large part to the fact that accord or harmony are to be grounded precisely in their opposites, that is, in the politics of discord and fragmentation: agreement on the word *prochain* is to be maintained, indeed defined, as violence to the conventions and presuppositions of ordinary language. "Demeurer d'accord de ne point expliquer le terme" is at bottom to block the circuit of communication by which entry into the *demeure,* into the community—as defined by these two groups—is to be gained.

Having broken through to the machinery behind the once mysterious term; having penetrated the *dessein,* which is both the intent and structure of the anti-Jansenist activity, Montalte then puts that machinery and design into even more garish light. He is to do this in three important passages that come in quick succession. In the first of these, the phonological tactics are played off a larger question of peace in the Church. Pascal argues that even should the censure of Arnauld take place, the hostilities and confusion would hardly come to a happy end. Indeed, they would likely spring more vigorously as the conspirators rush to claim credit for Arnauld's demise; and in this rush of sectarian egos clambering for top billing, the repressed element—meaning—would *naturally* reinject itself back into the debate.

> Car, quand on aurait décidé qu'il faut prononcer les syllabes *pro chain,* qui ne voit que, n'ayant point été expliquées, chacun de vous voudra jouir de la victoire? Les Jacobins diront que ce mot s'entend en leur sens. M. Le Moyne dira que c'est au sien; et ainsi il y aura bien plus de disputes pour l'expliquer que pour l'introduire. (Letter 1, p. 41)

The reappearance of the *signifié* would come despite, indeed because of, decisions taken to require the pronunciation of the syllables *pro chain.* Montalte's analytical fragmentation of the Molinist password provides the reader with a visual point of reference with which to complement the conceptual meaninglessness of a term reduced to an isolated physiological act, to the production of sound.

This act of expelling air will have as much validity as the blank space, the dead air, separating the two syllables on the page. Approached from a different angle, Pascal's analysis would in fact "regenerate the differential process of meaning." Such is the view of Philip Lewis who, in an important examination of dialogic impasse in the *Provinciales,* engages in an ingenious disseminatory reading of this passage. Lewis proposes that the splitting of the term *prochain* into syllables not only underscores the ideological disunity of the Molinist side, it also invites a consideration of the syllables themselves as carriers of supplemental meaning: *pro/chain* can be read as "semically remarking" the linking of the two factions: *pro* = for; *chain* = chain. The term *prochain* would in Lewis's reading bristle with meaning insofar as it points to the Molinists' intention to "affirm power (victory) by controlling language."[3] It might also be said that this term devised to torment the Jansenists—which is the point Pascal is trying to make in his analysis—is also the device, the chain, with which the Molinists would at once lock the doors of the sanctuary and fetter their ideological enemies to the term, the state (*terme*) and the stake of heresy.

In any event, Pascal, not at all ready to give up one of his trump cards, will continue to pressure the Molinists' terminology by specifying even more garishly its phonological inflation. He exiles their adherence to that singular aspect to the realm of the nonsensical. If, as he predicts, both camps of conspirators will hold that the expression *pouvoir prochain* is to be understood in their own particular sense, and thus realize the fear of Le Moyne's disciple that they "recommencent leurs brouilleries," the evident and public result will be a fundamental disarming of the term, since for Pascal its danger can only be a function of the meaning it is supposed to carry. For a term to be noxious, it will first have to satisfy certain semiotic and semantic requisites. Otherwise, it has value only as noise: "il ne peut nuire que par le sens." A senseless term is one that cannot, at least in principle, reach its linguistic or political target since it floats randomly rather than in the direction (*sens*) of common usage and accord. Having made what is intended to pass for an incontrovertible distinction between sensible discourse—where signifier and signified, words and things, linguistic principle and semantic convention are supposed to relate to each other—and nonsensical noisemaking, Montalte once again poses the fundamental question: "Enfin, mes Pères, dites-moi, je vous prie, pour la dernière fois, ce qu'il faut croire pour être Catholique?" The response, damningly inappropriate to the issue of meaning and to the skew of the question just posed is this: "il faut, me dirent-ils tous ensemble, dire que tous les justes ont le *pouvoir prochain,* en faisant abstraction de tout sens: *abstrahendo a sensu Thomistarum, et a sensa aliorum theologorum.*"

In obvious contrast to the verb Pascal had used ("croire"), a verb targeting the specific issue of meaning, the Pères—and it is not only comical that they respond "tous ensemble" in the manner of docile schoolchildren or of thoroughly rehearsed flunkies, it is part of the point Pascal needs to make—maintain categorically that to be Catholic is to *say* that all the just have this proximate power. Belief has been transmuted into an act of speech only vaguely consonant with the speech act, "credo," expressing and reaffirming adherence to the precepts that define Catholicism. Pascal's "pères" do not maintain, even minimally, the semantic course or *sens* of Montalte's question. They do not, for instance, respond that in order to be a Catholic one has to *believe* that the just have this power. Indeed, anything resembling meaning is to be abstracted ("en faisant abstraction de tout sens"), that is to say, in keeping with the etymological resonances of the Latin verb *abstrahere,* isolated, dragged off, excluded; which, incidentally recalls the effect the term *pouvoir prochain* had on Montalte when he first heard it ("ce terme me jeta dans l'obscurité"). But just as that initial "violence" was quick to show itself as contrived and rhetorical, so too is this violence of abstraction. Indeed, it is to be deflated completely, by what amounts to an abstracting of the abstraction. Pascal would have his reader believe that the Molinists have actually turned to Latin in order to give an even greater sense of authority to their position; but the Latin he gives them, made up of easily decodable cognates, serves the opposite purpose. It renders the foolishness of the message it carries even more foolish, precisely by spotlighting it as an empty act of speech playing burlesquely on the surface—sound and fury signifying nothing.

This is underscored even more forcefully in Montalte's immediate response. In contrast to the Molinists' tempest in the teapot of abstraction, where the exiling of meaning would appear to portend meaning, Montalte situates the act of speech on an even more superficial plane—more superficial than the "dire" of "il faut dire que les justes ont le *pouvoir prochain...*"; more superficial than the "appeler" of "s'il appelle ce pouvoir..."; more superficial than the "prononcer" of "quand on aurait décidé qu'il faut prononcer les syllabes *pro/chain.*" Now it is literally a matter of lip service to the magic word: "il faut prononcer ce mot des lèvres de peur d'être hérétique de nom." In effect, Pascal has taken the Molinists' abstraction one step further: he has isolated the requisite speech act on the lips; he has specified this act as a physiological gesture disjoined from any meaning other than its own articulation. It is, of course, not without interest that Montalte parallels his modification of *prononcer* ("des lèvres") with a similar modification of the heresy linked to a refusal to pay the appropriate lip service. This heresy would be nominal ("de peur d'être hérétique de nom"). It would be predicated on the same substantial lack as the term that defines it and would, we can infer, take its place among the Molinists' linguistic weapons.

Montalte makes an important push to isolate—to abstract—the term by posing a series of pointed questions regarding the provenance of the expression *pouvoir prochain.* To each question in which is posited a traditional source of authority (e.g., scriptural, patristic, and Thomistic), the massed respondants are forced to answer in the negative, a response which, on the theatrical or phonological level of the *Lettres* themselves, may be seen as ironizing the consequences of not paying lip service to the magic word, insofar as the repeated "non" homophonically negates the credibility of this "hérésie de *nom.*" It is perhaps more than coincidence that the "non," intoned three times, recalls Peter's stubborn, bad-faith denial of Christ. While the allusion may be associative, it can nonetheless be justified to the extent that the point of departure for this tussle over proximate power had in fact been the Molinist reaction to Arnauld's interpretation of Peter's fall, that is, of his triple denial of his association with Christ.

By the end of the letter, the repeated negatives and the rejection of any authority and inherent sense of the terms will be turned over to Montalte's fictional *destinataire* and transformed into a pretext for charity: "je vous laisse cependant dans la liberté de tenir pour le mot *prochain* ou non; car j'aime trop mon prochain pour le persécuter sous ce prétexte." The *mot barbare,* that is, the word standing outside the frontiers of the linguistic community of which both Pascal and his adversaries are supposedly members, is in this final analysis to be remembered as a pretext for persecution. In qualifying the Molinist linguistic strategy as a pretext, he underscores in no uncertain terms the complicitous nature of their designs. A pretext is defined as a deflective measure put into place in order to mask true motives—a fairly accurate account of Port-Royal's view of the Molinists. Their activity would be pretextual in another sense as well. The terminology they employ, this mysterious or magic word, circulating outside the conventional linguistic track, also stands outside the official texts (Montalte has already forced his adversaries to admit that scripture and other authoritative texts offer neither doctrinal nor semantic precedents for such terminology). Indeed, while not a single reference to books or other written material is made in his letter, no effort has been spared—at least in the fiction that Pascal creates—in pointing to the purely vocal, "pre-textual" features of the critical terminology. What Pascal does then in his uncovering of all this linguistic chicanery is to remove the expression from the pre-textual, that is, hidden and conspiratorial environment where it purportedly functions as if part of normative theological discourse, and plant it in the soil of a text, a supposedly naive letter to a friend, in order to show just how foreign it is to that discourse, as well as to common sense. Of course, the textual soil of this letter has been tainted so as to ensure that the word flourish garishly before dying an appropriate death. That death— in a manner of speaking from overexposure—is accelerated in the end by yet another dose of Pascal's own phonological gameplaying. In the closing moment of the letter, the reader can perceive an undeniable abundance of the phonemic elements that could be considered the signature of the expression being gutted. At the very minimum, that sound, [p], most prominent in "j'aime trop mon prochain pour le persécuter sous ce prétexte," sounds on no less than ten occasions in the final two sentences of the letter. By reducing the word, itself previously reduced to syllables, to an even more minimal constituant, and by hammering that sound home at the very close of the litiginous letter, Pascal is able to highlight even further the phonocentric plasticity and substantive vapidity of the word.

If, on the other hand, this concentration of the telltale consonant is purely coincidental to the terms employed, it is surely no coincidence that Pascal keeps his stranglehold tightly about the neck of his adversaries as he launches into the second letter where another expression, *grâce suffisante,* is to be submitted to the shock of his probing. We learn *en un mot* that what distinguishes Jesuits (this mention marks the Order's nominal début in the *Provinciales*), Dominicans, and Jansenists is their orientation to the notion, or more appropriately, to the term *grâce suffisante.* The orientations of the various communities parse out in this manner: the Jesuits hold that a grace is given to all men who of their own will determine its efficacy. This grace is called sufficient. The Jansenists, unshakeable partisans of efficacious grace, see this sufficient grace as redundant in the face of the stronger and unfailing efficacious grace. Finally, the Dominicans or neo-Thomists, hold to what is characterized as a most bizarre position. Improbably, they agree simultaneously with the Jesuits and the Jansenists. On the one hand, they concur that it is efficacious grace, not distributed globally, that determines the will to act, *but* that this grace in fact acts as a supplement to sufficient grace, universally given, but apparently unequal to the task of moving its host's soul to action.

Montalte and M.N. are quick to pronounce this sufficient grace insufficient by definition, insisting that it already contains the element of its own semantic negation: "si elle suffit, il n'en faut pas davantage pour agir; et si elle ne suffit pas, elle n'est pas suffisante" (Letter 2, p. 44). Based on the wisdom gained from the lessons of the first letter, Montalte will exhibit little surprise upon hearing that all men receive sufficient grace. This does not seem to be his immediate interest. He exploits, rather, the point that the Jacobins say it without thinking it. Obviously, the differential between thinking and saying is critical to Pascal/Montalte's objectives, not only with regard to doctrinal issues, but also to the behind-the-scenes maneuvering of the anti-Jansenist forces. It will be essential to show that the numerical superiority of the Jesuit-Jacobin alliance is at bottom nothing more than numerical; and that, since such superiority is predicated on fraudulent linguistic convention, any censure of Arnauld coming as a consequence of that convention will also be fraudulent. To get at this fraudulence, Pascal knows he has to strip the alliance of the cement holding it together. That cement goes by the name *grâce suffisante*. The stripping is to take the form of an analytical assault designed to demonstrate that *grâce suffisante,* like *pouvoir prochain,* is a phonological monstrosity, not a valid theological construct.

Montalte's opening move is to suggest that the Jesuits, master politicians that they are, will not engage the Dominicans in doctrinal discussion, even though the substance of the issues would seem to warrant such engagement. To the contrary, the Jesuits are shown as willing, even delighted, to settle for a quiet acceptance of the expression *grâce suffisante* on the part of their traditional rivals: "Les Jésuites se contentent d'avoir gagné sur eux qu'ils admettent au moins le nom de *grâce suffisante,* quoiqu'ils l'entendent en un autre sens" (Letter 2, p. 44). The accusation is loaded with semantic barbs intended to deflate any illusions of equality with the Jesuits that the Jacobins might entertain, as well as to poke at the contrived use of a term loosed from the moorings of common sense. Pascal insists, for example, that "elle" [la Société de Jésus] se contente d'avoir gagné sur eux," thereby suggesting that the Jesuits will accept a *pis aller,* a compromise solution. The point is this: when, as is the case here, politics reign, what the Dominicans *think* is of distant importance. What counts, what are to be counted, are their voices, deputized to transmit the agreed upon terminology and, it may be assumed, to tow the Jesuit party line in the proceedings against Arnauld. Pascal further enhances the political patina of all this by using the verb *gagner:* he wants his readers to understand that it is a matter of *rapports de force;* and he wants his other audience, the Dominicans themselves, to come to the humbling realization that, while their numbers may be decisive, they are of trifling consequence on an intellectual or conceptual level. This is made even clearer in the verb Pascal chooses next: "admettre." The Jesuit annexation of the Jacobins will have succeeded if the Thomists can be moved to admit the name *grâce suffisante.* It is evident that admitting falls to the shy-side of authentic conviction. Indeed, Pascal rhetorically manipulates the reader in order to oblige him to see in the Dominican acquiescence an intellectual compromise shamelessly tolerating, despite philosophical adherence to another sense of the term, nothing more than the name of *grâce suffisante.* And this other sense, now internalized and plowed under by the victorious Jesuits, is quite different from mere acceptance of the term as presently used and understood; it would be something like a real, even if conceptually questionable, meaning. It is therefore to the Jesuits' advantage to cultivate the Dominicans' "complaisance"[4] on this matter in order to present the look of a solid line of defense against Jansenist incursions into the inner sanctum of a Church undergoing what to Jansenist eyes is a dangerous and error-ridden process of modernization. This complacency is identified later in the letter as a yielding to the Jesuit juggernaut. According to the hapless Dominican plaintiff, the Jesuits had gained impressive momentum early on in their counter-reformational program and, by exploiting the ignorance of the public, had managed to sow the doctrine of sufficient grace "en peu de temps" and "avec un tel progrès, qu'on les vit bientôt maîtres de la créance des peuples, et nous en état d'être décriés comme des Calvinistes" (Letter 2, p. 49).

Now, if Pascal/Montalte had predicated his reading of the political motives and linguistic maneuverings behind *pouvoir prochain* on that term's apparent lack of meaning, or on the obstinate use of the term while refusing to divulge its meaning, the attack on *grâce suffisante* will hone in on what would pass for meaning. Pascal has his fictional operatives make repeated references to the general public and to its understanding of the word *suffisant,* which, as commonly held, can only denote something like the criteria necessary for action. From another angle, Pascal argues that the Jesuits will have won—once again he rubs the Dominicans' faces in the notion of an unhappy power relationship with the Jesuits—by treading lightly on the Thomists. In effect, they would not be required to deny the notion of efficacious grace. The reason for this good will and this victory is that "le monde se paye de paroles." The world contents itself with words in the same way the Dominicans "admitted" to the Jesuits' term. The world does not think to question a term it has no reason to suspect is being used outside the conventions of common usage. On yet another occasion, Montalte will ask his Dominican interlocutor if in taking his vows ("en quittant le monde") he has not forgotten what the term "sufficient" used to mean. Such recourse to the court of public authority serves not only to underscore and do further violence to the phonological isolation of the term as uttered by the Molinist conspirators, it also points to the dissemination of faulty terminology to an unsuspecting, if not wholly unsophisticated, public.

Following this analysis, Pascal will try to show that Molinist investment in the phonological is not limited to a technical point of theology, but marks in a significant way the censure of Arnauld. In this regard it is of some interest to look quickly at the "Réponse du provincial aux deux premières lettres de son ami." This response, placed between the second and third letters, sings of the near-universal acceptance of the preceeding letters:

> Tout le monde les voit, tout le monde les entend, tout le monde les croit. Elles ne sont pas seulement estimés par les théologiens; elles sont encore agréables aux gens du monde, et intelligibles aux femmes mêmes. (p. 52)

The praise heaped on the first two *Lettres* by the "provincial" respondant as well as by two sources he quotes serves Pascal's design in an important way. Not only does this praise underscore the popularity of the *Lettres,* and in so doing, look to generate even more popularity, it also provides some insight into why the letters are so popular. One of the sources quoted in the response, thought to be Madame de Scudéry, in evaluating one of the *provinciales,* points to the fact that it is well written; that it narrates without giving the impression of narrating; that it clarifies some of the thorniest problems; that it makes light in a refined way; that it is instructive and pleasurable; that it constitutes an excellent apologetic text and provides a clever and innocent censure. It is against this backdrop of critical praise that the "respondant," who may, of course, be Pascal himself, addresses the issue of the inevitable and imminent censure of Arnauld.[5]

When at the end of the response Pascal has the provincial friend exhort Montalte to continue producing the letters and to let the censure come "quand il lui plaira," he may be looking in two directions: back to the first two letters and on to the letters to follow. The backward glance is manifest in the friend's language: should the censure come, the Jansenists will be ready for it since the offensive linguistic weapons, *pouvoir prochain* and *grâce suffisante*, having already been dismantled, "ne feront plus peur." Moreover, the lessons concerning the anti-Jansenist cabal have already been mastered: "Nous avons trop appris des Jésuites, des Jacobins et de M. Le Moyne, en combien de façons on les tourne, et combien il y a peu de solidité en ces nouveaux mots pour nous en mettre en peine." Pascal is thus able to provide (for himself) an unsolicited, uncomplicated résumé and reassertion of the salient features of the initial letters.

At the same time, the response from the provincial orients the reader in the direction of the next letter by preparing the terrain from a new angle (of course, the angle has in a sense already been fixed with the censure of Arnauld, a censure that is placed somewhere in the future).[6] That new angle uncovered in the vivisection—or autopsy—of the Molinists' vocabulary is the censure itself which now has come "quand il lui [a plu]"; but since it had been predicated on the menace contained in *pouvoir prochain* and *grâce suffisante,* it can be said to have already been defused. So the censure can be picked apart with the same intellectual tools as the controversial terminology. In other words, it need not translate as a crisis or as cause for panic; it need not put the Jansenists on the defensive or on the run. And if Montalte expresses surprise—"elle m'a extrêmement surpris"—his astonishment comes from the disequilibrium between expectation based on past experience (the Jansenists had been painted in the blackest light as schismatics, as cabalists, as factionals, and as purveyors of error) and fact (the censure apparently does not jibe at all with the gravity of such accusations).

The censure, like *pouvoir prochain* and *grâce suffisante*, is to be viewed more as a problem to be analyzed, explained and, most of all, exploited. It is therefore not surprising that, in the richness of Pascal's analysis, a phonological element not substantially different from the kind marking those magical terms is exposed. After having gone through the theological points purportedly at stake (the case of Saint Peter, who in

Arnauld's view would provide a clear example of a just man from whom grace was withheld on a particular occasion) Montalte finally gets around to his punch line on the subject of the censure: for whatever reason they might have held, the Molinists *"n' ont fait autre chose que prononcer* ces paroles: cette proposition est téméraire, impie, blasphématoire et frappée d'anathème et hérétique." The censure would, in this view, be located in the same phonological wasteland as the terms devised to precipitate it. Cut off from any sense other than that of affixing political orientation, the censure can be portrayed as a litany of bald imprecations to be transmitted by boisterous public reiteration of its terms. It is very much to Pascal's purpose to give the impression that the force of the censure resides in its stridency and repetition, not in its appropriateness. In short, what he does here is to take the actual words of the censure, make sure the reader sees them as the consequence of bald chicanery, and then insist on the misleading "logic" of forceful public proclamation. The repeated voicing is, in Pascal's view, designed to win over an innocent and unquestioning public:

> Leur censure, toute censurable qu'elle est, aura presque tout son effet pour un temps; et quoiqu'à force d'en montrer l'invalidité il soit certain qu'on la fera entendre, il est aussi véritable que d'abord la plupart des esprits en seront fortement frappés que de la plus juste du monde. Pourvu qu'on crie dans les rues: "Voici la censure de M. Arnauld, voici la condamnation des Jansénistes," les Jésuites auront leur compte. (Letter 3, p. 58)

And this *compte* they are to have will come from the natural tendency on the part of the public not to read the text of the censure, to believe the shouts in the street; and if they do read it, not to understand what they are reading, nor to see that it is inadequate to the substance of the issues being debated.

It is clear that Pascal's intent is to isolate the censure, to precipitate it out of the larger discourse, and to show it is alien to reason, sense, evidence, and due process. In effect, he would have his readers see it as foreign to the very qualities of his own letters denouncing the censure and its presuppositions. He wants, in fine, to qualify the censure as a close cousin of the phonological gibberish taken to task in the preceding letters. Moreover, the cry in the streets is to have the same rhetorical status and effect as a mysterious envelope of silence in which the anti-Jansenist forces choose to wrap themselves: master politicians, the Jesuits and their allies enhance the boisterous censure by turning to the eloquence of silence.

Taking the attitude of "we have spoken and what has been said has been said," the Molinist forces would exploit "leur plus sûr parti [qui] a toujours été de se taire." In other words, just as they had "démeurés d'accord de ne point expliquer ce mot de prochain et de le dire de part et d'autre sans dire ce qu'il signifie," they will shroud the censure in proprietary mystery, letting it stand as accusation and indictment whose conclusiveness will neither allow for counter-argument nor demand further precision. "Ce silence même est un mystère pour les simples et la censure en tirera cet avantage singulier, que les plus critiques et les plus subtiles théologiens n'y pourront trouver aucune mauvaise raison" (Letter 3, p. 59). The censure is to bask in silence; it is to be insulated from the naive and the lettered alike.

Correlative to the matter of the censure is the whole issue of heresy which too will manifest some of the phonocentric features Pascal ascribes to the policies, actions, and intentions of his adversaries. The charge of heresy is, of course, not a trifling one. It is the ultimate accusation leveled in the defense of fundamental theological principle. As such it carries the most serious connotations and threatens the most serious consequences, namely forced separation from the body of the Church. Nor is heresy a simple "textual" or thematic concern for Pascal. By the time he is enlisted to lend his mind, his pen, and his sense of the world to Port-Royal's cause, the Jansenists have already been associated officially with heresy. From the very outset, the cloud of heresy is one under which Pascal is obliged to operate, and which he will have to dissipate. If the immediate pretext for the composition of the *Lettres* is to rally support for Arnauld, the larger issue in which Arnauld's case is implicated is the increasing threat to Port-Royal and the fundamentalist theology it espouses. To fail to clear the air on this issue would not only have an apparent impact on the privilege of Augustinian theology, but would leave the anti-Jansenist forces at a distinct theo-political advantage within the Church. On frequent occasion, then, Pascal will punctuate the *Provinciales* with this pressing issue of heresy.

Characteristically, his initial approach to the subject will be as indirect as it is vigorous. Rather than argue in a manifest way against the charge, he will take a rhetorical position that presumes it to be a given, and will then manipulate it as part of his own argumentation. This enables him to underscore even more emphatically its inappropriateness. In the first letter, one of the rhetorical assumptions under which he operates is that the Jansenists are already "heretical": "s'il appelle ce pouvoir *pouvoir prochain* il sera thomiste et partant catholique, sinon il sera janseniste, et partant

hérétique" (p. 41). By conjoining heresy and Jansenism in this way, Pascal
is able to accomplish two things en route to re-establishing what he wants
understood as the truth of the Jansenist position. First, he situates the
Jansenist "heresy" in the same bath as the Molinists' linguistic chicanery:
the supposed heresy and the use of the term *pouvoir prochain* are in a direct
functional relationship with each other. Consequently, the analytical dismantling of the disputed terminology and its magic powers would also
obviate the force of the accusation. The simultaneous deflation of the term
and the charge attached to it is, as we have seen, made clear in the causal
link between noncompliance with the enunciation of *pouvoir prochain* and a
"nominal" heresy ("Vous le direz ou vous serez hérétique de nom"). The
second advantage of this tactical conjunction is of a similar, but more
general, and public, nature. In effect, the reader will have to ponder the
question posed implicitly by the logic of Pascal's maneuvering: is it
possible to consider as heretical someone who, for reasons that satisfy the
demands of linguistic common sense, refuses to subscribe to and utter
terminology that is at the very minimum controversial? Of course, Pascal
will see to it that the reader comes to conclusions favorable to Port-Royal's
view. The reader will naturally deduce that the anti-Jansenist forces have
not understood the criteria for determining heresy; or, more damningly, that
they have in fact understood them and have opted all the same to base
accusations on criteria wholly inappropriate to the issue.

In the second Letter, Pascal ups the rhetorical and argumentative
ante. The dispersing of the cloud of heresy will not come as a simple
linking of nonsensical terminology to "nominal heresy." He will, rather,
twist things in such a way that if the Jansenists are to be considered heretical
for their position with regard to the terms and the concept of *grâce
suffisante,* so too are the Jesuits.

> Où en sommes-nous donc? m'écrirai-je, et quel parti dois-je ici prendre?
> Si je nie la grâce suffisante, je suis Janséniste; si je l'admets comme les
> Jésuites, en sorte que la grâce efficace ne soit pas nécessaire, je serai
> "hérétique,"[7] dites-vous. Et si je l'admets comme vous [he is
> addressing the Dominicans], en sorte que la grâce efficace soit néces-
> saire, je pèche contre le sens commun, et je suis "extravagant," disent
> les Jésuites. (p. 46)

It is important to note that Pascal is not engaging here in a round of name
calling; nor does he baldly accuse his adversaries of heresy. What he does

is to place the terminology upon which they themselves insist into a larger frame. He factors that terminology out to the logical ends demanded not by the words but by what the words define. In so doing he is able to saddle his adversaries with the consequences of their language as it might be understood by anyone disposed to understanding it, not just pronouncing it. Dogged subscription to the term *grâce suffisante* will in effect tie the Jesuits to a logical, linguistic, and doctrinal stake. The illogic and falsity of the terms designed to exile the Jansenists are made to ricochet back onto the purveyors of falsehood. There is here the underlying sense of something that will become a more explicit point as the letters progress; namely that truth will have its way, that untruth will eventually and inevitably be destroyed by its own momentum towards contradiction.

In Letter 3 Pascal continues in his effort to clear the air with regard to the purported heresy of the Jansenists. If, in the first two, he had managed to spotlight the bizarre criteria used by the Molinists for imputing heresy, and had even been able to catch the Jesuits in the prison house of their own language, he will now show how the heresy of the Jansenists has nothing whatever to do with the ordinary sense of the term. He will show that the Molinists have in fact sired an entirely new kind of heresy, one manifesting some of the features of the magic word. As in the case of that word, where form and *pro-forma* agreement were everything, the *new* heresy would have nothing to do with the substance of things. In the view Pascal needs to promote, doctrinal orthodoxy would no longer be the principal issue. It is not the message that is heretical, it is the messenger:

> Ce ne sont pas les sentiments de M. Arnauld qui sont hérétiques; ce n'est que sa personne. C'est une hérésie personnelle. Il n'est pas hérétique pour ce qu'il a dit où écrit, mais seulement pour ce qu'il est M. Arnauld. C'est tout ce qu'on trouve à redire en lui. Quoi qu'il fasse, s'il ne cesse d'être il ne sera jamais bon catholique. (Letter 3, p. 60)

The heresy that the Molinist cabal would ascribe to the Jansenists is at bottom a mutation of the very notion of heresy, a monstrosity that, in Pascal's words, will not let go its prey until that prey dies. And just as there are certain animals with which one is ill-advised to wrestle, Pascal does not make explicit moves against this beastly charge. His task had been to bring the monster out into the open and to identify it. Having done this, he lets it loose and turns it on its Molinist masters. Secure in the feeling that it will gnaw and tear appropriately at its creators, Pascal has Montalte walk away and dismiss the heresy as "imperceptible."

With the change in focus initiated in the fourth Letter—the Jesuits and their moral precepts are about to become the specific target of Pascal's activity—the matter of heresy is given a slightly different cast, the whole thing being treated as some sort of joke. In this letter it is a question of whether or not, as the Jansenists maintain, a feeling of remorse is not inevitable each time a sin is committed. In the Molinist view such a sentiment would unfailingly be provided by God. Pointing to the obvious case of libertines, atheists, and idolaters, Pascal paints the Jansenists as convinced that a sense of guilt can in no way attend each temptation to sin. From this angle, the Jansenists would be deemed heretical. Whereas in the earlier letters Pascal had Montalte cleverly work the issue of falsely imputed heresy and leave much of the judging to the reader, he now has Montalte come right out and dismiss the charges as laughable: "C'est une assez plaisante chose d'être hérétique pour cela."

A similar posture will be taken in Letter 15. There Pascal produces material that garishly spotlights the thinking of the Jesuits on this most serious issue. In effect, he has unearthed what amounts to a corollary to the "personal" heresy laid out in Letter 3. If Arnauld could be singled out as something like heresy become flesh, the Society of Jesus itself is now shown to be something like orthodox doctrine become flesh. To make the point, Pascal has come up with the case of a certain Monsieur Puys. It seems that this Puys had translated a book—Pascal deems it an "excellent livre"—regarding the duties of Christians faced with prelates who would turn them away from their obligations. Although the text in question treats the matter in a polite and general way ("sans user aucune invective, et sans désigner aucun religieux, ni aucun ordre en particulier"), the Jesuits see themselves as singled out for criticism. Their virulent response, confected by a Père Alby, not only accuses Puys of stylistic impropriety (he is deemed "scandaleux par ses galanteries") but also declares that he is impious, heretical, excommunicable, and fit for the fires of hell (Letter 15, p. 205). However, when Puys eventually specifies that his text, which is in fact a translation, treats the question in a general way, that it does not target the Society of Jesus, and that he himself has a great deal of respect for the order, the same Alby who, on two occasions, had attacked him in books qualified as "sanglants," now writes of him as "un homme d'esprit très éclairé, de doctrine profonde et orthodoxe, de mœurs irrépréhensibles."

Pascal's outrage erupts at this meeting of contradictory discourses, themselves representative of an implausible contradiction in Puys himself. How, Pascal asks, is it possible that Puys be at once pious and impious, irreprehensible and excommunicated, catholic and heretic "sans qu'il se passe aucun changement en lui"? In this contradiction lies the essence of the issue; for the retraction shows that the original condemnation of Puys was made en *connaissance de cause*. The two quotations provide clear textual evidence of a falsified, thoroughly biased use of the term. From this Pascal can infer that the term "heretic" circulating forcefully in so many Jesuit pronouncements ("tant de personnes catholiques y sont appelées hérétiques")—must also denote this specialized heresy of "attacks against the Jesuits." For the Jesuits to accuse the Jansenists of heresy can be legitimately understood as something like "we deem you worthy of excommunication and damnation for the simple reason that you speak against our order." This "theo-logic" equating attacks against the Jesuit order with heresy is, in the broader lines of Pascal's argument, borne out in the Jesuits' moral positions. One of the principles of the excessive casuistry promoted by the Jesuits is the primacy and persuasiveness of human or earthly appetites, themselves specific manifestations of the more fundamental demands of self-love. It is this *amour-propre*, this need to work always toward the satisfaction of one's own interest, that would supposedly justify the conjunction of anti-Jesuit sentiment and heresy. Pascal puts it as a "truth" of psychology that applies with special appropriateness to the Jesuits:

> L'Amour-propre nous persuade toujours assez que c'est avec injustice qu'on nous attaque; et à vous principalement, mes Pères, que la vanité aveugle de telle sorte que vous voulez faire croire en tous vos écrits que c'est blesser l'honneur de l'Eglise que de blesser celui de votre Société. (Letter 15, p. 204)

In the early letters, Pascal tries to deflate the accusations of Jansenist heresy by showing them to be focused exclusively on the personality and the unshakable "guilt" of Antoine Arnauld. By the later letters, it is not just Arnauld but all of Port-Royal that is targeted. Indeed, the words "Port-Royal" will themselves be invested with the phonological aspect of the Molinists' magic words. At one point, for example, Pascal protests that his task will not be to prove the innocence of the nuns at Port-Royal, but to prove the maliciousness of their Jesuit detractors. And part of the defense he makes is that his defense will itself be rejected precisely because he himself will be perceived as being from Port-Royal.

> Vous ne manquerez pas néanmoins de dire que je suis de Port-Royal; car c'est la première chose que vous dites à quiconque combat vos excès: comme si on ne trouvait qu'à Port-Royal des gens qui eussent assez de zèle pour défendre contre vous la pureté de la morale chrétienne. (Letter 16, pp. 216-17)

Just as *pouvoir prochain* and *grâce suffisante* had been designated as passwords for orthodoxy, "Port-Royal" has become an infallible index of heresy, insofar as it resumes in Jesuit eyes all inflections of anti-Jesuit sentiment. And since "Port-Royal" stands as the functional equivalent of "heretic," the latter term will have a same operational value as the former.

The magical, exclusionary features invested in the term "Port-Royal" carry naturally to its synonym, the word heretic itself. In Letter 17, Pascal addresses himself directly to the king's personal confessor, François Annat, S.J., who had recently published a response to the *Provinciales* entitled *La Bonne Foi des Jansénistes en la citation des auteurs*. In exposing the "logic" of Annat's accusations, Pascal makes the following argument. The author of the letters is presumed to be from Port-Royal; as far as the Jesuits are concerned, Port-Royal has been declared heretical; from which it can be inferred that he who writes the letters can and must be declared heretical. This conclusion will not have derived from standard criteria for determining heresy, criteria that Pascal specifically demands:

> Je vous demande quelles preuves vous en avez. Quand m'a-t-on vu à Charenton? Quand ai-je manqué à la messe et aux devoirs des Chrétiens à leur paroisse? Quand ai-je fait quelque action d'union avec les hérétiques, ou de schisme avec l'Eglise? Quel Concile ai-je contredit? Quelle constitution de Pape ai-je violée. Il faut répondre, mon Père, ou... vous m'entendez-bien. (Letter 17, p. 235)

Since the word heretic has been appropriated into the Jesuits' lexicon of magic words, it only has to be uttered to take on the contours of reality. Like the other magic words it only has to be pronounced in order to generate substance out of nothing. It only has to be enunciated and all substantive argument would be blocked. "Car vous dîtes *que, pour toute réponse à mes quinze lettres, il suffit de dire 15 fois que je suis hérétique, et qu'étant déclaré tel, je ne mérite aucune créance"* (Letter 17, p. 234). The Jesuits' presumption of control over language and the numerological bias of their thinking would, in a sense, have come together in this radical effort to suppress the invisible voice that refuses to be suppressed. Not only has the charge itself become an automatic, knee-jerk response, it will also be depicted as a movable or substitutive value. Pascal wants it plainly understood that the Jesuits' accusations of heresy follow changes of circumstance. Pascal puts it this way:

> [...] malgré tout ce que je viens de dire, vous n'avez pas cessé de publier qu'ils [the Jansenists] étaient toujours hérétiques. Mais vous avez seulement changé leur hérésie selon le temps. Car, à mesure qu'ils se justifiaent de l'une, vos Pères en substituaient une autre, afin qu'ils n'en fussent jamais exempts. (Letter 17, p. 240)[8]

Along with the issues of the censure and the accusations of heresy is a larger, more basic, and more damning charge concerning the Jesuits' misuse of language; namely, slander. Now, the issue of slander is a rich one in the *Provinciales,* and it is one that shows the Jesuits wanting their cake and eating it too (but perhaps in the end, choking on it). On the one hand, unflattering intentions and pronouncements against the Society of Jesus are automatically considered slanderous and therefore heretical. On the other, the casuists themselves maintain in their manuals that to engage in calumny against one's enemies is no sin. Pascal will take full advantage of the damaging implications of this position; not, of course, by turning to it for "authorization" to slander the Jesuits, but by exploiting its obvious self-destructive feature. To this end, he will not content himself with a point by point cataloging of his adversaries' calumnious positions. Armed with a principle that will allow him to cut more quickly to the heart of the issue, he declares that he will "passer plus avant" (Letter 15, p. 202). This move into the deeper reaches of slander is a move into an area privileged by casuist thinking, namely, intention.

> Je ne ferai pas voir seulement que vos écrits sont remplis de calomnies, je veux passer plus avant. On peut bien dire des choses fausses en les croyant véritables, mais la qualité de menteur enferme l'intention de mentir. Je ferai donc voir que votre intention est de mentir et de calomnier; et que c'est avec connaissance et avec dessein que vous imposez à vos ennemis des crimes dont vous savez qu'ils sont

innocents, parce que vous croyez le pouvoir faire sans déchoir de l'état de grâce. (Letter 15, p. 202)

Pascal's analytical precision on the subject of calumny—he wants his reader to keep in mind that to slander is to tell untruths—effectively corners the Jesuits by showing them to be textually, and by their own admission, on the side of untruth. They are on record as saying in all truthfulness that recourse to untruth is permissible. The maxims legitimizing lies ricochet against the casuists perhaps even more forcefully than their other pronouncements. Indeed, Pascal targets the Jesuits' stance on language with these maxims. In their hands, and on their pages, language would be a mechanism to be twisted and deformed to suit political, self-promotional objectives. Moreover, and more importantly, this corruption of language serves to undermine deeply the credibility of the Jesuits. How can the proponents of untruthfulness be taken as proponents of truthfulness in other matters? Such is the position Pascal takes in Letter 16 where he underscores the obvious way in which the principle destroys the efficacy of the practice: "Mais en disant, comme vous faites, que la calomnie contre vos ennemis n'est pas un crime, vos médisances ne seront pas crues" (Letter 16, p. 231).

The use of language to attain untruthful ends finds a parallel on the more basic level of illicit or untruthful expropriation of words themselves. Throughout the *Provinciales,* Pascal will continuously try to box the Jesuits into a corner. More specifically, he will try to demonstrate by means of their own published opinions that they cannot be trusted to use language in ways conforming to the requisites of either the moral or social order. One of the most obvious and easily exploitable linguistic practices of the Jesuits is their readiness to transform words to fit the demands of a moral system that puts a premium on adaptability. The casuists will target for specific treatment words whose standard and commonly accepted meaning would, in effect, trap sinners in their sin. By changing the definition, the term is changed and, according to the kind of equational thinking Pascal attributes to his adversaries, so too is its sense and use in the real world. As the sense of the term changes, so too does the responsibility a person may have had for his actions. He or she would no longer have committed the action described in the standard but "outmoded" sense of the term. If, as the Jesuit voice is made to say in Letter 5, the Church Fathers were "bons pour la morale de leur temps; mais [...] sont trop éloignés pour la celle de la nôtre," so too are certain conventional and conservative definitions. Such, for example, is the case of the term *assassin,* which the casuist semanticists have defined in a way that effectively shifts things away from the substantive element of homicide and towards an ancillary one, namely, the financial. Assassination is no longer defined simply as murder, but specifically and strictly as murder by hire; and this aspect will have been refined to require an actual exchange of money as requisite for any consideration of moral responsibility. Killing in order to "obliger un ami" would no longer fall under the semantic embrace of the term "murder." In much the same way, dueling is permitted by changing the operative definition of the term itself.

An even more telling instance of this kind of interpretive assault on definition attends the issue of simony. Pascal explains the casuist urge to change the meaning of the term in this way:

> Comme vous vous êtes trouvés embarrassés entre les Canons de l'Eglise qui imposent d'horribles peines aux simoniaques, et l'avarice de tant de personnes qui recherchent cet infâme trafic, vous avez suivi votre méthode ordinaire, qui est d'accorder aux hommes ce qu'ils désirent, et donner à Dieu des paroles et des apparences. (Letter 12, p. 167)

The casuist thinkers, caught in the undertow of two antagonistic discourses, the moral and the worldly, opt to rectify the dilemma by redefining the terms upon which the Church had based not only its proscription, but also the "horribles peines" awaiting those who would ignore that proscription. The point Pascal wants to make, and one he makes on numerous occasions in the *Provinciales,* is that the excesses of the casuists are as much violations of language as of doctrine or religious principle. In the case of simony, the attack on language is necessitated precisely because a word, "simony," actually exists; and since it exists, there must be meaning attached to it. ("Mais parce qu'il faut que le nom de simonie demeure, et qu'il y ait un sujet où il soit attaché...") In deference then to the preexisting term and also to man's indomitable desire to realize a profit, in this case from the buying and selling of sacred offices, a new definition is derived for the word "simony," one that specializes the criteria to such a degree that the old sin of simony effectively vanishes. Indeed, the fact of simony would vanish so completely that not even Simon the Magician could be held accountable for the sin named after him. That definition, stipulating that the financial aspect may be considered the motive for, not the price of, the transaction, is qualified by Pascal as "disproportionée," as "imaginaire," as "méta-physique," and as a "songe." All these terms point to a course of action, to a "solution" falling completely outside the margins of standard linguistic expectation and practice. They point in effect to adherence to a fanciful language that has but the most tenuous rapport with the one used commonly by the various parties of this dispute.

The writer of the letters will show, moreover, that the Jesuit violence to linguistic convention is not just an isolated phenomenon. It would have been given the status of doctrine, as, for example, in the celebrated *doctrines des équivoques et des restrictions mentales,* close cousins of the doctrine of probable opinions and the direction of intention. The *doctrine des équivoques* first appears in the ninth Provincial and is advertised as a means of avoiding sin in conversations and in worldly dealings ("les intrigues du monde"). More precisely, it has been concocted, we are told, to legitimize untruth when one wants to pass untruth off without technically falling into a lie. To realize such improbable magic, the Jesuit theoreticians have come up with a method by means of which the economy of discourse can be simultaneously broken and kept intact. This method would permit the use of ambiguous terms "en les faisant entendre en un autre sens qu'on les entend soi-même." The operative element of this maxim is based on an implicit distinction between *faire entendre* and *entendre,* between what is received by the interlocutor and by what is transmitted to the speaker.

There is here, as there was in the case of the magic words, an inflation of phonological features. This inflation is contained in the verbs *entendre* and *faire entendre,* both of which signify intellectual acceptance, "understanding," and aural perception, "hearing." The speaker would have his interlocutor understand what he wants him to understand by having him hear something other than what he, the speaker, means; or as the French verb can suggest so aptly, what he "wants to say" (*veut dire*). There is, in short, a fragmentation or break in the communicational circuit—just as there had been in the semantic conventions to which Pascal appeals in his analytical investigation of *pouvoir prochain* and *grâce suffisante.* In both instances, the speaker violates what would be one of the basic conceptual axes of Pascalian thinking, the principle of univocity. The speaker, the one in a clear position of power with regard to his own discourse, is allowed to supplement the apparent sense of that discourse with a second meaning retained in the mystery of language "heard" only in the privacy of his intention, his desire, his *vouloir dire.* More precisely, the supplemental sense is camouflaged and transmitted on the wavelength of the listener's expectations, themselves based "naively" on the conventions of ordinary language. In the transmission of the message to the listener, the *vouloir dire,* carried by an ambiguous term, dominates, diverts, and transforms the *dire,* sending it on a vector that oscillates (the term ambiguous originally denoted a side-to-side movement) between the public or accepted meaning and the back alleys of private meaning. In other words, the game is being played, or better, the play is being acted out backstage. The play of ambiguity is solely the speaker's concern, for it is he alone who is aware of any ambiguity; he alone has access to the mutually exclusive paraphrases defining ambiguity.[9] And it is in this way that the lie is said to be avoided. The ambiguous language maintains enough semantic contact with correct or conventional meaning—with what might be called *le bon sens*— to keep the speaker just out of harm's way. The underlying premise here is that lying, apparently modeled on standard forms of communication (e.g., exposition, dialogue, interrogation, etc.) somehow demands the complicity—unwitting or unwilling as it may be—of the person being spoken and lied to. If the conventional circuit can in some way be disrupted, broken, or circumvented; if the listener does not "hear/understand (*entendre*) the lie being told him, the lie can in effect be said to evaporate. And with this evaporation of sin and culpability, both the embarrassment (the "social culpability") and the difficulty of avoiding the uneasiness of lying ("une chose des plus embarrassantes est d'éviter le mensonge") are subsumed by what to the recipient's ears would be conventional (truthful) discourse, but which to the speaker's "ears" carries an enhancement of that same language.

These notions of enhancement, anti-conventional discourse, and secret linguistic accommodation are even more evident in the maxim Pascal exploits next in this same letter. Indeed this new maxim, a more refined, less evident version of the doctrine of equivocal language, gives the theoretical model for yet another doctrine, that of mental restrictions. The maxim reads:

> On peut jurer [...] qu'on n'a pas fait une chose, quoiqu'on l'ait faite effectivement, en entendant en soi-même qu'on ne l'a pas faite un certain jour ou avant qu'on fût né, ou en sous-entendant quelque autre circonstance pareille sans que les paroles dont on se sert aient aucun sens qui le puisse faire connaître. (Letter 9, p. 129)

Here it is not simply a matter of avoiding public recognition of untruth, but of subverting a solemn speech act, the oath.

Whereas in the preceding maxim, where an oscillating word was pronounced to launch a complex and confounding sense, it is now more literally a question of "hearing." A magic formula completely distinct from the language perceived by the listener, is uttered by the speaker. The maxim suggests, for example, that the person making the solemn promise localize it in temporal structures ranging from the conceivable ("un certain jour") to the fantastic ("avant qu'on fût né"). The vanishing act at the heart of this maxim continues on into even more secretive reaches as *entendre* is transformed into *sous-entendre,* which if we be permitted to exploit momentarily the literal components of the term, seems to suggest that "hearing"/understanding has been rarefied to something even less palpable, to something like "under-understanding," to something heard even more faintly, less definably (the maxim refers, for instance, to "quelque autre circonstance pareille") than the temporal restrictions proffered earlier in the maxim.

This movement towards even more inaccessible reaches of the psyche is reflected in and "justified" even further by the broader doctrine of the direction of intention—a subject to be treated later in some detail. For the moment, suffice it to say that the intention claimed to define the quality of an action would, in the manner of equivocal language, serve to remove the action from the clutch of cause and effect logic and to situate it on the level of a pure and dominant subjectivity. But as if to suggest at this point that such evaporation of *entendre* into the darkness of intention is such a subtle or bold concept that it would not be taken seriously by his innocent readers, Pascal has his Jesuit propose another, more certain way to avoid lying: "et il [the casuist Filiutius] y donne encore un autre moyen plus sûr d'éviter le mensonge." In this other mechanism, the inflated phonological element is presented with scandalous clarity. One can, for example, modulate an oath in the following fashion: after clearly and distinctly pronouncing the performative formula—in this case "I swear [I didn't do such and such a thing]—the person giving his word can deliberately cause the performative to misfire by adding at low volume (*tout bas*) a temporal element ("today") that would in effect limit the operational scope of the oath and would consequently abrogate the promiser's obligation to be true to the word his interlocutor believes he has received.

A second example of this procedure is even more wily in that a speech act (the oath) is countered by another speech act ("que je dis") pronounced just out of earshot. The addition of the second element, syntactically subordinate to the initial element—it is a relative clause—ends up dominating the oath. What the recipient of the oath hears and understands is this: "I swear that I did not do this thing." What the purveyor of the oath *said* is this: "I swear *I say* I didn't do this thing." In point of fact, the speaker speaks a truth here, for he has in fact said what he says he said. He has uttered the magic (enough) formula and has, according to the provisions of the maxim, insulated himself from untruthfulness and perjury.

In a repeat performance of the tactic taken earlier, Pascal has Montalte raise the objection that such procedures may lie beyond the wit of most people. Not to be thwarted by such a mundane obstacle, the Jesuit counters by further removing the supplementary restrictions. The speaker would not be required to come up with an appropriate formula for the instantaneous abrogation of his oath. The magic is to be performed not by means of conditions tacked secretly to what is perceived as the giving of one's word, but by a formula concocted *in advance*. Not surprisingly, there is a fascinating proviso qualifying the use of the prearranged formula: the user must, as a general rule, *intend* to enhance his discourse with the sort of formulations a clever man, that is, more clever than he, would give to his discourse. So while the perceived component maintains a high level of visibility, the transformational component is drawn further into secrecy. It is removed further from the moment of the declaration itself. The bath of intention, in which the erstwhile "lie" of claiming not to have done something one is fully conscious of having done, has, to extend the image, been drawn well in advance: the person prone to turn to such tactics would, it is inferred, have already made the requisite comparison with the discourse of a clever man so as to guarantee the effectiveness of his own "unpronounced" discourse, and thus to guarantee that his intention to ape such discourse be founded on a model at least vaguely discernible to him. But as the Jesuit puppet suggests in his next statement, this "connaissance" is not always at the user's fingertips. Indeed, Pascal has his Jesuit ask Montalte if he has not often found himself in a tough spot for want of this knowledge ("manque de cette connaissance"). The question is playfully rich, for it may be asking either about knowledge of the maxim or about the knowledge of the lowest common denominator, that is, "the sense of the discourse of a clever man." Montalte is, of course, disposed to give the Jesuit more rope by affirming that he has indeed found himself in such a predicament. This edges his informant into further refinement of the maxim: whereas in the previous examples it had basically been a question of denying responsibility for an action one had in fact committed, it is now a matter of nullifying a promise yet to be made. The difference between the two cases may at first seem slight, but it is hardly without interest to the larger implications Pascal seems to be drawing from these maxims—that the sort of legitimized violence to the sanctity or reliability of one's word is not only morally repugnant, it also harbors grave social and political consequences. What Pascal wants his readers to sense—and what the attentive reader cannot help but sense—is that the casuist prescriptions threaten the social order based on the contractual giving of one's word, an order that would be the primary model of all human social structures.[10]

In the maxims Pascal associates here, there is a perceptible move from reaction to an act to the contamination of an act. If, in the earlier instances, an act, understood as criminal, sinful, or in some other way untoward, had been committed and subsequently denied, the denial served basically to deflect blame or to avoid embarrassment. As dishonorable as this refusal to accept responsibility might appear to Pascal—and through him, to the readers of the *Provinciales*—it does not yet pretend to abrogate the act itself. On the surface of things the act has real status in a real world. The act and its consequences are known, and this allows, at least in principle, for some sort of accommodation or response by the offended party. In the case of the promise, however, an open-ended context of expectation and anticipation is established. The recipient of the promise looks naively to the transformation into act of the word that had been given as bond. The maxim authorizing unspoken, unperceived abrogation of the promise maintains that "les promesses n'obligent point, quand on n'a pas l'intention de s'obliger en les faisant" (Letter 9, p. 130). It goes on to stipulate that "il n'arrive guère qu'on ait cette intention, à moins que l'on les confirme par serment ou par contrat: de sorte que quand on dit simplement: Je le ferai, on entend qu'on le fera si l'on ne change de volonté: car on ne veut pas se priver par là de sa liberté." The casuist attack on the promise targets the sense of obligation fundamental to the very notion of the promise. To promise is, by common understanding, to tie or oblige oneself to future accomplishment of the act specified at the moment of the promise and represented by the currency of the word put forward (*pro-mis*). It is also then to tie (*obliger,* from the latin *ligare* = to tie) the speaker as much to himself as to the one spoken to. Now, under the stipulations of this maxim, the ties that bind—or the bond that ties the promiser to the recipient of the promise—would no longer be in force, precisely because the ties with oneself, with the words "heard" in the internal discourse can be severed intentionally, that is, by directing one's intention.

Incredibly, violence to the social machinery based on a premise of being as good as one's word is taken even further. The same maxim is seasoned with a dose of what is supposed to pass for the authority of empirical evidence: rarely will men be prone to enslave themselves to their word (the maxim ends with that appeal to the imperatives of personal liberty). Now since the will is not likely to seek out the devices of its own ensnarement, there seems to be little reason to insist on it as a criterion for action. Consequently the maxim ends up stipulating that the promise ("je le ferai") expresses the likelihood of a future act (at which time "je le ferai" is transformed into "je le fais") only so long as one does not change his mind on the matter. Here again the critical verb "entendre" comes into play—"on entend [when one says 'je le ferai'] qu'on le fera si on ne change de volonté"—suggesting that this *entente* with oneself is still an aspect of the discourse one holds with oneself—a discourse predicated on intention, which is to say with something very much like desire itself. Indeed, the two terms, *intention* and *entendre,* already linked etymologically,[11] stand as fundamental elements of a program of morality that is itself co-extensive with theological positions reflecting exaggerated faith in the efficacity of human will.[12] And in the view Pascal wants to transmit, this allegience to the demands of the will, to desire, appetite, *amour-propre,* and self-interest is predicated on a fragmentation of linguistic structure, proper logic, and most importantly, the demands of *charité.* The Jesuits would have chosen the worldly path, the one leading naturally and by definition to confusion, capriciousness, and contradiction. They would have chosen the road of rationalization as opposed to the road of reason. Pascal will spare no pain in making this choice abundantly clear and onerous to his adversaries.

Chapter 3

Pascal's Tactics of Counterfragmentation

UP TO THIS POINT OUR ATTENTION has been focused ostensibly on some of the assumptions and practices defining the fragmentational activities of the anti-Jansenist forces. These activities, among which the rethinking of linguistic convention and liturgical practice, would be part of a wide-ranging and error-ridden agenda. At issue in this agenda would be man's place in the Church, the Church's place in the world, and, of course, the Jesuit order's high place in both: "Ils [the Jesuits] ont assez bonne opinion d'eux-mêmes pour croire qu'il est utile et comme nécessaire au bien de la religion que leur crédit s'étende partout, et qu'ils gouvernent toutes les consciences" (Letter 5, p. 73). As Marsha Reisler puts it so aptly, Pascal's objective, one that he realizes with undeniable effectiveness, is to ensure that "the reader emerges with a firm conviction that the Jesuit Society is a scheming political force in the act of undermining no less than the Christian tradition, the moral fabric of society, the classical aesthetic and the scientific and critical reasoning which the reader values."[1] To lead the reader to this perception and to move him to reject the theological and moral agenda of the Molinists, the author of the *Provinciales* will want to do more than simply submit the shortcomings and exaggerations of the Society of Jesus to the judgment of the public court. Nor by some sort of magisterial *fiat* will he want to condemn them. The exposition of Jesuit and casuist positions, while spectacular in its own right, is complemented by a second line of discourse, Pascal's response or counter-logic.[2]

Confronted with a sense that the unicity and integrity of the Church are in a state of clear and pressing danger, he is virtually obligated to respond to the evidence he presents, evidence that the casuistry deriving from Molinist presuppositions corrodes the basic principles of Catholicism.

And his response has to be as specific as the indictment made in the exposition. With regard to the fragmentational positions of the casuists, Pascal will provide an argument that is both entertaining and serious enough to counter the particular attractiveness of Jesuit positions responding often and favorably to wholly human appetites and impulses. In fine, his argument will look to fragment the casuists' fragmentation by rendering the whole less appealing than the sum of its parts and at the same time by isolating those parts as outlandish, indefensible, and often contradictory. To this end, the author of the letters adopts a responsorial strategy that attacks his adversaries' positions from the intersecting angles of analysis (dissolution) and citation (accretion).

The analytical voice is heard with special clarity in the early letters where the Molinists' magic language is singled out for special attention. It is very much in Pascal's interest to exploit before his reader's eyes an important premise: theological and political differences notwithstanding, he and his casuist adversaries can, in principle at least, be considered as operating on a common ground, namely, the language they both use. The issue, as Pascal opts first to present it, is less theology than it is French. Having every reason to believe—or, more aptly, having every reason to make a show of believing—that with the help of the common sense inscribed in the language they share, differences, even seemingly insurmountable theological differences, can be reconciled. Pascal responds to the fragmentational linguistic positions of the Molinists with a fairly conventional semiotic analysis. And although the outcome in the *Provinciales* of Montalte's theatrical and picaresque effort is never in doubt, Pascal takes his readers through the choreography of his agent's analyses in such a way that they are encouraged to participate in the discovery process. In so doing, the reader will be compelled to believe that Port-Royal's rejection of the Molinist language is entirely logical, deriving as it does from the fundamental structures and proper use of his own language.

In the case of *pouvoir prochain,* Montalte's efforts are, over the course of the first letter, directed at trying to extract from stubborn adversaries a working definition of a term that he had been forced to engrave in his memory, as his intelligence could not wholly grasp it. His efforts to comprehend the terminology, to encircle it, and thus bring it back into the fold of common linguistic and semantic structures, are based on an urge to re-establish the principles of fair play and common sense that the purveyors of this terminology seem intent on fragmenting. To this end, he turns to the common sense of ordinary language and the basic difference between a word and its referent. We should recall parenthetically an evident point, one that, given the persuasiveness of Pascal's fiction, it is easy to lose sight of: the author of the *Lettres* is the one who animates the adversarial voice. The Molinists, like the ventriloquist's wooden companion, only seem to speak. In the first ten letters at least, they are in fact only voices thrown by Pascal and made to say what Port-Royal needs said in "defense" of what, in the Jansenist view, are bizarre linguistic positions. And these positions will be rendered all the more bizarre to readers who cannot help but accede to the sensible qualities and feel of Pascal's argument.

In the face of stubborn "opposition," Montalte will exploit a categorical and easily argued distinction between the word and its referent: "je ne dispute jamais du nom, pourvu qu'on m'avertisse du sens qu'on lui donne" (Letter 1, p. 40). But the magic word, *pouvoir prochain*, constitutive element of an obscurantist plot, is made to hold solid against Montalte's analytical assault, so that all he can apparently do is to throw up his hands, not in defeat, but in profound, almost epic revulsion, as if this magic word were a kind of monstrous disease or curse inflicted on the peoples of the earth and on their language: "Heureux les peuples qui l'ignorent! Heureux ceux qui ont précédé sa naissance." In the end he calls upon the learned guarantors of the language, the "Messires de l'Académie" to banish from the Sorbonne this barbarous word that causes so much division and fragmentation.

In a move designed to amplify the syllabic splitting of the original magic word, *pouvoir prochain*, Pascal has Montalte and his Jansenist counsel submit *grâce suffisante* to an even more technical fragmentation:

> Mais, lui dit [the Jansenist], il y a deux choses dans ce mot de *grâce suffisante*: il y a le son qui n'est que du vent, et la chose qu'il signifie, qui est réelle et effective. Et ainsi, quand vous êtes d'accord avec les Jésuites touchant le mot de *suffisante*, et contraires dans le sens, il est visible que vous êtes contraires pour la substance de ce terme, et que vous n'êtes d'accord que du son. (Letter 2, p. 47)

At play here are variant articulations of the basic semiotic components, the signifier [Sa] and the signified [Sé]. For the sake of clarity it may be helpful to schematize the Jansenist argument:

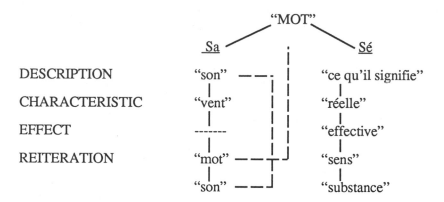

Immediately apparent in this schematization is a certain *defectiveness* on the side of the signifier [Sa]. If I underscore the term "defective," it is to emphasize a second, more literal sense in which to read it, namely, in its juxtaposition with, and opposition to, the "effective" of the "réelle et effective" appearing in Pascal's formulation. This "defect," which also constitutes the inherent ineffectiveness of the expression Pascal analyzes (*grâce suffisante*), manifests itself in two places. First off, what on the level of signification had been deemed "effective," has no counterpart on the side of the signifier. The implication of this absence is most fully appreciated by careful attention to the meaning of the term "effectif." The word denotes something that produces a real effect. That which is effective exists in reality.[3] In his semiological analysis, the Jansenist is then either unable or unwilling to recognize the productivity, the "reality" of the term he examines. Now, it is obvious that Pascal, who directs the "Jansenist's" hand in the service of Port-Royal's linguistic principles, cannot deny the actual existence of the expression *grâce suffisante*. It exists in and by its very articulation. What he does deny is the sense carried by the term as ordinarily understood and used. He cannot see how the term as it is being used by the Molinists can denote that which is real and productive. In other words, although he can make no argument against the presence of the word, and although he cannot refute the physical reality of "sound" and "wind," he can point to the absence of a referential constraint on that word. He can emphasize through his own witholding of a term and by his own tactical silence, the essential emptiness of a word without a tie to any reality other than its own production. This elusiveness is, of course, already suggested in the earlier evocation of "wind," that is to say, as the empty physical gesture of displacing air in the production of speech. It is, moreover, in direct diacritical opposition to *la chose qu'il signifie* that Montalte positions the term "wind," a term that already connotes meaninglessness and insignificance. The reader will automatically think of an expression such as *ce n'est que du vent.* To the extent then that *il y a le son qui n'est que du vent* means something like *il y a le son qui est insignifiant et vide,* the reader can infer that investment in the phonological aspects of the term *grâce suffisante* produces only emptiness. This lack is highlighted in Pascal's argument by the diacritical blank coming after *vent.*

A second instance of defectiveness, not unrelated to the *vide* of the first, can be seen in the turning of Pascal's vocabulary back upon itself. Here again the symmetry and orderliness of the pairings break down. This time, however, the defect is not one of emptiness and silence. It comes, rather, as a repetition, as a return to the point of departure, that is, to the very notion of the word itself. As indicated in the schema, in its original state the *word* represents a unity which then undergoes analytical bifurcation into terms marking the signifier and the signified. At the critical point where some kind of complement to *sens* is demanded, Pascal purposefully reintroduces that original term, "le mot"—quand vous êtes d'accord avec les Jésuites touchant *le mot* de *suffisante*, et contraire dans *le sens...*" The interest of this stylistic "lapse" into redundancy resides specifically in what the Jansenist semiotician recognizes to be a parallel defect in the terminology he criticizes. The purported significance of such terminology lies in its self-significance. The meaning (*sens*) of the Molinist's term is limited to a circumscribed, encapsulated self-reflexivity—to a return onto itself. This movement or direction (*sens*) does not point outward to an absent referent, but rather inward towards what, in the wake of Derrida, might be termed a present refer*ant.* The *mot de grâce suffisante,* being insufficient in its effects (both as a theological concept and as a meaningful semantic entity), can only refer back to itself. Such is its *sens,* such is the course it takes. The action of the expression *grâce suffisante* is a kind of self-perpetuating reaction in the present. It is an action stranded in the moment of its articulation. Indeed, Pascal wants his readers to sense that it is only as mere speech production that the terms can, and are supposed to, operate. Their signifying function is limited to marking the political and theological position of the speaker, and not to remarking an absent referent.

Pascal's appreciation of this phenomenon of phonological presence and substantive absence is underscored by another "defect" in the symmetry of his argument, by the fact that *son* appears in exactly the same sequence as it had initially; that is, directly after "mot." As such it establishes a cyclical, that is, fundamentally unproductive and sterile structure. The Molinist term simply turns in place; it turns in on itself to become magical. Finally, it is significant that the redundant use of the term *son* appears as the diacritical alternative to "substance," to that aspect of the sign which stands below (*substare*), waiting to be brought back to the surface, to the present. This representational ineffectiveness of the refusal to recall an invisible but virtual *sens* continues to situate the conspiratorial activity in the redundant present.

As suggested earlier, this recourse to semiotic analysis, if it is aimed at the exponents of error, must operate on the assumption, fictional or sincere, that analytical argument can bring the adversary to his senses; in this case, to commonly held presuppositions on language and its use in the real world. Of course, this may not at all be the case in the early letters. The good sense of Pascal's analysis may in fact be constructed more for public consumption than for the intellectual rehabilitation of the Molinist cabal. Pascal's public relations task is as much to show the common sense and analytical propriety of Jansenist thinking as to effect what would be an almost miraculous change of heart by key opposition figures. The commonsensical, logical argument Pascal deploys serves ultimately to portray the Molinists as charlatans operating in a self-serving environment bearing little cousinage either to normative codes of language *or* orthodox theology. The analytical tactics—or ploy—that Pascal engages in may end up pointing to the ultimate "futility of conversing in incompatible languages—and thus to the impossibility of meaningful dialogue."[4]

If, on the face of the fiction Pascal creates, there appears to be an impasse, this does in no way signal defeat. Pascal will let his analyses stand their ground and make their points to an increasing number of readers. The impasse does signal the advent of a shift in the direction that the investigation and exposition are to take. The analytical process is not abandoned, it is given different trappings. If, in the early letters, that process had been focused on relatively narrow linguistic and technical issues, in the letters to come, it will target the language of the Jesuits as it appears in the wider world of their published opinions.

Since Pascal's business, especially in the sequence of letters dealing with Jesuit opinions on morality, and in his rebuttals to the Jesuit protestations of mistreatment and deception, is as much editorial as it is polemical, as creative as it is factual, we can, and should, talk of how he arranges it to the best advantage of his cause. In short, we can talk of the rhetorical and stylistic strategems to which he resorts and to which we can attribute the durability of a work that from a literary and compositional point of view remains as fascinating today as it was some 350 years ago. In this regard we can talk not only of the technique, but also of the thematic of counterfragmentation. Rightly or wrongly, Pascal and his compatriots at Port-Royal saw in the casuist project a fundamental assault on sacred tradition, precedent, and practice. In the face of this assault, the authors of the *Provinciales* will want to persuade the public that Molinism, Jesuitism, and casuistry constitute a fully operational system that has to be dismantled. The principal tactic for this dismantling will be to fragment his adversaries' system precisely by what amounts to an integrative gesture; namely, by showing the Jesuit theology and moral teachings as internally correlated and as coherent in intention, if not in effect. His principal reserve of weapons will be the Jesuit texts themselves, and his major tactic of sabotage will be the collage. If in the early letters he made use of fictional representatives of the schools he was attacking, namely the Jesuits and the Dominicans, and if in those letters the discourse of those puppets was fictionalized, in the letters on morality that same fictional discourse, voiced by a Jesuit "mouth"—he is little more than that—will be supplemented by a factual discourse coming from the casuist handbooks on morality, a discourse that from the Jansenist perspective represents a fictionalized, fanciful, and fundamentally corrosive view of Catholicism.

This aspect of the *Provinciales* begins in Letter 4. By this time, the censure of Arnauld has, as expected, come down from the Sorbonne. Fortified nonetheless by the indisputable success of the initial *Provinciales*, the Jansenists see no reason to abandon the advantage they hold in the public forum. Indeed, it is incumbent on them to increase the pressure, and it is in this spirit that Pascal opts to leave behind the theologians' disputes to take his case elsewhere. If the anti-Jansenists cannot, for example, distinguish or reconcile doctrine with the purveyor of doctrine—the condemned propositions would, according to M. Le Moyne, "be orthodox in any mouth other than Arnauld's"—they can no longer be deemed worth the letter writer's time, precisely because they give him no satisfaction in his need for sensible answers to his queries and objections. And if he continues on his picaresque romp through the thickets of illogical positions, it is to provide a properly garish introduction to the feature presentation. By the fourth letter, composed a month after the first, the time has come to get to sources. Montalte wastes no time coming to the point: "Il n'y a rien tel que les Jésuites" (Letter 4, p. 61). They are the model, the generating force behind the confusion and cross-purposes left behind on the ninth of February, 1656, with the close of Letter 3. Indeed, the fourth letter, coming some two weeks later, would represent a very clear transition from the purely theoretical—*grâce actuelle*—to the more juicy and exploitable issues of casuist thinking on morality on which the Jesuits can be said to have written the book. And the "Jesuit" whom Pascal has Montalte visit is in a sense the word made flesh—or fleshy. He is a handy and naive personification of a seemingly unrelenting series of quotations from the books of his fellows, their sympathizers, imitators, and commentators. In short, Pascal has left the uncontrollable confusion of too many confused voices to visit the very controllable confusion of primary source material.

    If in the opening paragraph of Letter 4 he belittles the disciples of the Jesuits, he is also suggesting that the copying in which he himself is about to engage will be something far less approximative and confused. Indeed, his is to be the work of a scribe reproducing on paper the texts before his eyes. It is perhaps important to mention in parentheses that virtually from day one a debate has simmered as to whether or not Pascal was in fact faithful in his scribing. Not surprisingly, the Jesuits who responded directly to Pascal's accusations (Nouet, Annat, and eventually Daniel) all maintain that he was not playing fair, that he had truncated, decontextualized, or blatantly misrepresented their texts and intentions. This same charge is raised by Roger Duchêne, who sees in Pascal's work the construction of a system where there is none.[5] Other scholars, perhaps best represented by Louis Cognet, have determined that, with remarkably few exceptions, Pascal was true to the letter and intent of Jesuit teaching. The debate over whether or not Pascal was an editorially faithful scribe or whether he was a biased hatchet man bears a marked resemblance to the kind of controversy that had surrounded the matter of the five propositions. Some say the propositions were textually in the *Augustinus*, others say not; and others maintained that the decontextualized propositions betrayed the spirit of Jansenius's argument. Suffice it to say that the jury is still out, and promises to remain out, on this aspect of the *Provinciales*. It is probably prudent, then, to steer clear of these especially treacherous waters by limiting the present investigation to the artfulness (or artifice) of Pascal's response, to how he manages a convincing *mise en scène* of the Jesuit material he makes speak so decisively against itself, how, in short, he fragments the Jesuits positions by conjoining their material and by situating it within a discourse designed expressly to highlight its aberrant qualities.

It is in the fifth Letter that Pascal first draws his readers into the strange and fascinating world of Jesuit moral theology; and as this fifth Letter serves as an initial and exemplary instance of his method, I will examine it in close detail. If the first three *Provinciales* leave the Jesuits reeling by making hash of alliances formed to deal with Antoine Arnauld, the block of letters, numbers 5-10, where the invisible, determined, and terribly clever adversary lays into that Society's moral and theological writings, must have positively horrified them. This is all the more understandable in that Pascal arranges things so that the wounds would be wholly self-inflicted. The Jesuit texts are to be transformed into instruments of torment against their exponents. To arrive at this objective, Pascal will take the following rhetorical positions: 1) he will valorize his letter as the locus of reliable information, thereby giving the impression of an impartial forum for the discussion to follow (it is, of course, nothing of the sort); 2) he will establish a perceptible and appealing context of "fairplay," even "charity," allowing him to explode the Jesuit texts with grace and wit; 3) he will engage in a strategy of citational work by means of which he will orient the casuist precepts in ways that fairly well guarantee that a cooperative—or co-opted—reader can do no other than accede to the Jansenist position.

Standing pertinently as precedent to the cut and paste job Pascal is to perform on the Jesuit texts—and Society—are two works. The first is the *Théologie morale des jésuites*, which has been described as "une lointaine origine d'une campagne qui prendra son plein dévelopement 13 ans plus tard avec les *Provinciales*."[6] In this text, Antoine Arnauld, with the collaboration of François Hallier (later to take up the Jesuit side) launches a serious and systematic attack on Jesuit moral teaching based on the doctrine of probabilism. For all its seriousness, however—and doubtless because of it—Arnauld's text is generally lacking in seductiveness. Now, if seduction was not one of the author's preoccupations, persuasiveness surely was; and the very weightiness of Arnauld's case seems to have worked against that objective. His argument and references may have been accurate, his cause just; but it all bogged down in the anesthetic effect of some 150 instances of Jesuit chicanery piled on top of each other; and Arnauld's brass tacks commentary only added to the reader's burden.

The second text against which the letters on casuist morality could be read is much more proximate and suggests an internal rationale for the tactics Pascal is to deploy against the Jesuits. In fact, it is the third *Provinciale* where Pascal, in violent reaction to the fresh censure of Arnauld at the Sorbonne, tries to manipulate public opinion with assertions that the judgment was more the result of a patchwork of assenting voices than of just cause and proper argument: "il leur est plus aisé de trouver des moines que les raisons." In like manner, he will train his rhetorical spotlight on the suite of imprecations contained in the censure. He does this by asking, or rather, by having the supposedly bewildered public he represents ask:

> D'où vient [...] qu'on pousse tant d'imprécations qui se trouvent dans cette censure, où l'on assemble tous ces termes, de poison, de peste, d'horreur, de témérité, d'impiété, de blasphème, d'exécration, d'anathème, d'hérésie, qui sont les plus horribles expressions qu'on pourrait former contre Arius, et contre l'Antéchrist même, pour combattre une hérésie imperceptible, et encore sans la découvrir. (Letter 3, p. 56)

The verb Pascal uses to characterize the censure is of special interest. This verb, *assembler*, promotes the idea of a forced, biased, and, it is suggested, false grouping. Just as he would have his readers believe that the censure itself had been railroaded through the Sorbonne on the basis of a quantitative mismatch—Franciscan monks, technically ineligible to vote, had been recruited for the proceedings—he would also have us accede to the Jansenist view that the censure itself hammers its point home by collating and boisterously announcing a suite of "les plus horribles expressions." This assemblage would seem to fit, moreover, into what Pascal wants recognized as a wider politic of anti-Jansenist activity. According to Montalte's interlocutor, the censure, censurable though it may be, would doubtless be received by the public as intended, at least for a while, and would, in Pascal's view, be part of an ongoing and pernicious campaign of political dirty tricks designed to keep anti-Jansenist sentiment percolating in the public consciousness:

Ils [the Molinists] vivent au jour la journée. C'est de cette sorte qu'ils se sont maintenus jusqu'au présent, tantôt par un catéchisme où un enfant condamne leurs adversaires, tantôt par une comédie où les diables emportent Jansénius, une autre fois par un almanach, maintenant par cette censure. (Letter 3, p. 58)

It is, then, in relation to these two texts, Arnauld's *Théologie morale des jésuites* and Pascal's own report of the other side's tactics of assemblage that we approach the letters on casuist moral policy. Now, Pascal will not want to fall into the same stolid rythms of his predecessor and collaborator. If Arnauld had systematically ordered and numbered what he calls his "échantillons," if he had arranged them under tidy headings, Pascal will purposefully fashion them into a multivoiced rhetorical collage. His most important tool will be a pair of scissors—not the literal ones he is to use in the preparation of the *liasses* of the *Pensées*, but literary ones to isolate quotations with which to fashion the main body of the collage. Roger Duchêne refers to Pascal's technique as one of montage—and the term is surely apropos. I prefer, however, its close cousin, collage, which all the while maintaining the notion of assembly contained in Duchêne's term, puts equal stress on the cutting up of an existing text, in this case, the Jesuit handbooks on morality. Moreover, by taking into account the juxtaposition of a diversity of elements to form a new text, the term collage invites us to consider this new text as a site of textual, topographical, and topical confrontation. As Alain-Michel Boyer points out in an article entitled "Les Ciseaux savent lire," the collage would be "un lieu stratégique où s'affrontent des lectures et des langages,"[7] which would be a fairly accurate description of what Pascal has in mind in his appropriation of the Jesuit texts. Is the author of the *Provinciales* not saying in effect, "all right, let us see how your language stacks up against my language, one that I can show to be an extension of the sacred language of scripture and tradition"?

On this point, it is essential to remember that Pascal and his associates are very much in the driver's seat, since it is they who already know to what end they would use the items culled from the casuit sources. It is they who, to use once again Boyer's thinking on the collage, "ne cess[ent] d'anéantir la continuité du texte," —the text in this case being the collection of casuist manuals—by interrupting and mutilating it. By privileging certain fragments, they, the Jansenist plaintifs, transform those aberrant fragments to the advantage of their own theological and political postures.

Letter 5 opens by drawing immediate and clear attention to itself as fulfillment of a promise made at the end of the preceding letter, thus cultivating in the reader a sense of the letter as guarantor of truthfulness, and consequently, of truth: "Voici ce que je vous ai promis; voici les premiers traits de la morale des bons Pères Jésuites." The deictic expression, *voici*, repeated in this first sentence emphatically announces the text under the reader's scrutiny as a point of reference, as having the weight of *evidence*; that is, as standing directly before the eyes (*videre*: to see). And the first parcel of evidence, exhibit A, concerns the character of the defendants. Obviously Pascal will want to call attention to what he thinks to be his adversaries' want of goodness, but will not want to jeopardize the methodological "reasonableness" of his position at this critical point in the letter by coming out simply with direct accusation. He opts then to explode the "virtue" of those whom he refers to as the "bons pères Jésuites" by citing it, by underpinning it with textual support. Seamlessly glued to the insinuation of the Jesuits' "goodness" is an element transforming it first into *sagesse* and then into *sagesse divine*: "voici les premiers traits de la morale des bons Pères Jésuites, de ces hommes éminents en doctrine et en sagesse qui sont tous conduite par la sagesse divine, qui est plus assurée que toute la Philosophie." This characterization would, of course, be measurably less potent coming directly from Pascal; that it comes from his adversaries themselves serves to sharpen its ironic edge, as, at the same time it corroborates the letter writer's implicit but clear claim of reliability.

Textually, this revelation of the Jesuits' "sagesse" stands as that first "trait" of their morality. And one should not discount the fact that the term Pascal uses, "trait," signifies not only a characteristic or trait, but also something drawn (*tiré*) from another source. (In a sense Pascal is going to milk—*traire*—the Jesuit texts in order to draw sustenance from them for the body of his own text.) In any case, the first "trait" he puts on the page, the first line he draws, is to show the Compagnie de Jésus as wholly full of itself. He breaks his quoting, however, to make an essential point—and it is this: his activity is not to be taken lightly or as comical: "Vous pensez peut-être que je raille: je le dis sérieusement, où plutôt ce sont eux-mêmes qui le disent dans leur livre." Indeed, Pascal says it seriously because he quotes seriously. His telling, his *énonciation* is serious because it is a precise replica of the Jesuits' own telling; and their telling is no different than the thing they tell, the *énoncé*. Pascal's *énoncé* is, of course, quite different— and the difference is based precisely on the transformational force of the collage he fashions. Cut from the pages of an ornate volume celebrating the centenary of the order and pasted onto the page of what is supposed to pass for a personal, if not wholly naive, letter, the quote is changed from a formula of praise and self-congratulation to the opening gambit of an inculpation. The transformational energy is provided by various protestations of seriousness, of faithfulness to the source, of precise scribing pasted between the lines of his quoting. "Je ne fais que copier leurs paroles; il faut les croire puisqu'ils le disent" (Letter 5, p. 72). In fine, Pascal has carefully laid the foundation for subsequent accusation and indictment by establishing the Jesuits not as liars, but as true to their word and therefore as eminently quotable.

In addition to Montalte himself, the Jesuits he will cite and the "Jesuit" who speaks in the letter, there is another who is true to his word: the friend who accompanies Montalte on the visit. Montalte tells us:

> J'ai voulu les [the Jesuit maxims] voir eux-mêmes; mais j'ai trouvé qu'il n'avait rien dit que de vrai. Je pense qu'il ne ment jamais. Vous le verrez par le récit de ces conférences. Dans celle que j'eus avec lui, il me dit de si étranges choses, que j'avais peine à les croire.
> (Letter 5, p. 72)

Montalte then goes on to make a provisional "defense" of the Jesuit order which he would claim to see as misrepresented by the vagrant voices of a few individuals. He further protests that he can counter his friend's examples of "jésuites relâchés" with his own examples of "jésuites sévères." This defense is, of course, only a pretext to open onto one of the fundamental issues of the letter, that is, the spirit of the Society: "Ce fut sur cela qu'il me découvrit l'esprit de la Société, qui n'est pas connu de tout le monde, et vous serez peut-être aise de l'apprendre. Voici ce qu'il me dit."

"Voici ce qu'il me dit." We have then a third voice in the rhetorical collage. The friend who never lies has as role the transmission of fact; it is he who, unlike Montalte, has already sorted out the theoretical under-pinnings and political imperatives of the Jesuits' activities. It is from the friend that Montalte, who plays the same role as the reader of the letters, first hears the term "doctrine des opinions probables." Now, in Pascal's text these terms, while appearing in the flow of the friend's sentence, are italicised; they can be read as a quotation. By drawing special attention to, by rendering more visual, the element it enhances, the italicizing of the expression "doctrine des opinions probables" would at once provide a textual simulacrum of the Jesuits' shamelessly public cultivation of the doctrine of probabilism—we are told that "ils ne la cachent à personne"— and trigger an indictment of it; for the act of quoting, and here I think more specifically of the French verb *citer,* is, in its origin, to call before a jury, before the tribunal of justice. In that "court appearance" the doctrine of probabilism is to lock horns with tradition and law. It is therefore no coincidence that Pascal provides this tradition with a similar graphic enhancement. What we read in italics is this: "la loi du Seigneur, qui est sans tâche et toute sainte, est celle qui doit convertir les âmes." The juxtaposition of these two "citations" thus provides a visual index of a fundamental confrontation between a doctrine, probabilism, whose basic component, opinion, is grounded in something less than certitude, and a law defined as pure, thoroughly holy and whose power and function are linked to the conversion of souls. In a very real sense the two italicised elements represent the two languages, the two discourses that, to recall Boyer's imaginitive characterization of the collage, Pascal will set against each other in mortal combat.

At this point of the letter, the friend who never lies—and who also never pulls his punches—sends Montalte out to confront the Jesuits and their books. Resonating in his exhortation, "allez donc, je vous prie, voir ces Pères," is a clear parody of the quotation Montalte had used in the opening paragraph of this letter, a quotation lifted from that tome celebrating the Jesuits' centenary. Now, that quotation, "allez anges prompts et légers," exhorting the Jesuits to disperse and assume their proper missionary role in the world, is itself already a quotation expropriated from Hebrew scriptures. And when Pascal quotes the Jesuits, when he quotes the quoting of a quote, he makes no effort to hide his ironic intent; nor does he resist the urge to underscore the contrived, self-serving use of prophetic utterance when he quips: "la prophétie n'en est-elle pas claire?"

The transformation of "allez, anges prompts et légers" into "allez donc, je vous prie, voir ces Pères," would be one more case in an extended declension of quotes—there are no less than six quotational moments imbedded in the text: the original utterance of Isaiah the prophet; the scripting of that utterance onto the scroll or page of scripture; the Jesuit expropriation; Pascal/Montalte's appropriation; the friend's transformation, which Montalte ends up quoting in the section of the letter falling under the lead sentence "voici ce qu'il me dit." This declension, underscoring the misappropriation of prophetic discourse and of Church history and tradition, ends up recuperating the tradition originally represented in that utterance. This is to be accomplished in large part by carrying the reader towards, and preparing him for, direct confrontation with a spiral of aberrant reworkings of traditional positions on ethics.

Unlike Arnauld before him, Pascal will orchestrate his confrontation with the Jesuit texts in a way that would engage the complicity of his reader. This complicity derives in part from the agreeableness the text is able to generate; and part of the pleasure Pascal seems to want to offer to the reader's perception is that, for all the seriousness of the analytic project at hand, his is not a witch hunt or a case of sectarian vengefulness. Of course he will want all bases covered, so if through the friend he can voice a relentlessly harsh view ("vous y verrez les vertus chrétiennes si inconnues et si dépourvues de la charité, qui en est l'âme et la vie, vous y verrez tant de crimes palliés, et tant de désordres soufferts [...] Comme leur morale est toute païenne..."), he can also have Montalte "counter" with a pose of charity and civility. It should, of course, be said that this sort of rhetorical jockeying is not at all ancillary to the designs of the polemic. Indeed, it is precisely this in-between-the-lines material that constitutes one of the components of the textual collage. Indeed it is the thing that differentiates the *Provinciales* from Arnauld's *Théologie morale des jésuites*, itself more specifically a montage than a collage.

Following the friend's prodding, Montalte goes and renews acquaintance with "un bon casuiste de la Société," whose greetings he accepts as if from a dear friend, and whom he first walks through a number of indifferent, unspecified topics in order to question him on the subject of fasting, itself a way to "entrer insensiblement en matière." Now, this *insensible entrée en matière* is an especially important aspect of Pascal's collage work. Not only does it underscore a gradual, almost disarming methodology—one that is in a sense analogous to the "reasonable," evolutive nature of casuist thinking, where one relatively innocent ruling serves as precedent for more outrageous and scandalous positions—it might also be considered paradigmatic of the larger activities of the rhetorical collage. It serves also to let the reader in on the secret and on the joke. In so doing, Pascal/Montalte galvanizes the circuit of complicity with the reader who, for his part, can revel in each turn of the screw.

"Venez à la bibliothèque." Come to the books, to the source of what you seek. The Jesuit's invitation is accepted without the slightest delay: "j'y fus"; and the first book that Pascal and his collaborators, both real

(Arnauld and Nicole) and fictive (Montalte and the Jesuit puppet), open to public scrutiny is Escobar's *Théologie morale*, a book especially appropriate to the theme and practice of the collage, since it is itself a compilation of material from no less than twenty-four Jesuit thinkers. Indeed, in response to Montalte's query as to the identity of this Escobar, the Jesuit indicates (indicts) him specifically as the one who compiled the *Théologie morale*. By stressing the communal nature of this work, Pascal is already able, without having to say as much, to extend the margins of the inculpation to include the Company generally and not just one aberrant voice. Nor is it without interest that the first quote lifted from the *Théologie morale*—and here we have a rather clear echo of tactics employed at the beginning of the letter—be one in which the Jesuits themselves are portrayed as incarnations of scriptural discourse, in a sense, as fleshed-out quotations. In this quote, an allegorical reading from the Book of Revelation, the twenty-four Jesuit sources of the *Théologie* would represent the twenty-four elders, while the four named Jesuits (Suarez, Vasquez, Molina, and Valentia) would incarnate the four creatures flanking the throne of God (*Book of Revelations*, Chapter 4). And if, as Cognet notes, Pascal, like Arnauld before him, resists the temptation to exploit the obvious comedic options open to him in the Jesuit bestiary, he does not let the matter go without comment. Rather, he remarks offhandedly that the allegory is sufficient to give him "une grande idée de l'excellence de cet ouvrage," thus implicitly putting into question from the very outset the ability of Escobar to provide persuasive interpretation and, one may construe, serious moral pronouncement.

Characteristically, Pascal does not tip his hand and manifestly debunk the maxims at this point. He is, rather, content to let them sabotage themselves and to totter under their own weight—with, of course, some additional prodding from Montalte. For example, while moving through a short series of maxims on fasting, continuing his "entrée insensible en matière," the question arises as to whether or not it is permitted to take wine while fasting. Not surprisingly, casuist thinking would allow the practice. "Peut-on, sans rompre le jeûne, boire du vin à telle heure qu'on voudra, et même en grande quantité? On le peut, et même de l'hypocras." Now, just as valuable to Pascal's project as the main part of the maxim authorizing virtually unlimited consumption of wine during periods of obligatory fasting is an addendum permitting the taking of hippocras or mulled wine. The usefulness of this detail is fairly evident; but as if to make sure that the suggestive term does not slip past the reader's notice, Pascal draws special attention to it; not only by having his Jesuit repeat it, but also by having him enter it dutifully into his collection of useful minutiae ("je ne me souvenais pas de cet hypocras [...] il faut que je la mette sur mon recueil") and secondly, by having Montalte infer without any provocation from his bewitched interlocutor, "voilà un honnête homme qu'est Escobar"; and it is at this point that the implicit phonological synapse *hypocras/hypocrite* is made.

For the Jesuit, however, Montalte's "complimentary" remark is irresistible encouragement to up Escobar's stock even further: " 'Tout le monde l'aime', répondit le Père." The reason for this universal affection? "Il fait de si jolies questions"—a clear cue to truck out even more outrageous maxims; which is precisely what Pascal/Montalte sets to do. He is not, of course, about to give up a good thing by blurting out something to the effect that he now has the Jesuit(s) where he wants him/them. He continues rather down the same path, taking his time to make sure that the readers do not get the impression that it is a question of a few isolated aberrations. He is having too much fun playing in the mud—mud with which he is purposefully and deliberately forming the walls of an edifice, the prison house of Jesuit language, a structure or system made of a dispersal of quotations and opinions. He then sharpens his focus on this rather banal matter of fasting. The maxim he exposes, given as a prime example of one of Escobar's "jolie questions" is a hair-splitting, technical operation that, very much in tune with quantitative thinking that will characterize the casuists' thinking in the *Provinciales*, determines that 1) someone in doubt as to whether he is twenty-one years old is not required to fast; 2) if a person is to turn twenty-one at one in the morning on a fast day, he is not required to fast, thanks to that space between midnight and one in the morning. Clearly Pascal presents this maxim not so much for shock effect. His citational strategy calls on him to *plaire* as much as *instruire*, so a quote such as this is exploited to amuse his readers at the expense of the casuists who, at this point,are portrayed more as silly and inconsequential than as scandalous and dangerous. In this spirit he has his two agents, Montalte and the Jesuit share a moment of almost schoolboyish glee: "O que cela est divertissant! lui dis-je. On ne s'en peut tirer, me répondit-il; je passe les jours et les nuits à le lire, je ne fais autre chose." The image of the Jesuit burning the midnight oil and the midday sun, gleefully pouring over these tasks is not simply comedic as it points to the self-satisfaction and pleasure with which the Jesuits view themselves; it also serves to underscore the self-reflexive, self-serving circuit characteristic of Jesuitical casuistry.

The pleasure that the publicizing of the casuit maxims gives to both Montalte and his Jesuit dupe encourages the latter to wade more deeply into the mire through which he is unwittingly being lead. "Le bon Père, voyant que j'y prenais plaisir, en fut ravi, et continuant..." (Letter 5, p. 77). In the succeeding maxim, the subject of fasting, following the program of the "entrée insensible en matière," picks up an aspect that effectively and seamlessly moves things into more scandalous areas. It is now a question of whether or not fasting is required if one has exhausted oneself in the pursuit of a woman. The answer is, of course, no—even if one has taken up the pursuit simply and expressly to work up the appetite that would make fasting incommodious.

At this point, Montalte finds himself in a position to bring a potentially more damaging issue into focus, namely the near-occasions of sin. As with the technicalities of fasting, the casuists have arranged things in such a way that what common sense used to term a near-occasion of sin is no longer an operational principle, especially when personal convenience is at stake. Upon hearing this, Montalte once again expresses pleasure: "Je m'en réjouis, mon Père" (p. 77). The reader is, of course, quite attuned to the real nature of this pleasure. It is, on the one hand, a tactical pose by which to prod an ever more delighted Jesuit to speak the words that will help ensnare his order. On the other, it is Montalte's genuine pleasure at seeing his own plan work so smoothly. Indeed, the *entrée insensible* that Pascal exploits is a tactical analogue to the inexorable and outlandish logic Pascal wants his readers to see in the concatenation of casuist prescriptions. And Pascal's own concatenation reflects rhetorical positions that transform the "pleasure" of seductive poses, designed to stimulate the Jesuit, into the genuine pleasure Montalte can express when his dupe, having swallowed the bait, arrives finally, and as planned, at the true *matière,* the *matière brute,* or clay, with which the edifice of casuistry is to be reconstituted in earnest.

As soon as the Jesuit voice provides the rationale for going against his own conscience with regard to the deliberate searching out of near-occasions of sin; as soon as he utters the magic words, "doctrine des opinions probables," which he qualifies as the "fondement et l'A B C de toute [leur] morale," Montalte has him. "Je fus ravi de le voir tombé dans ce que je souhaitais" (Letter 5, p. 78). The Jesuit has fallen into the trap, as he has fallen down to the level of the foundation upon which the exaggerated casuistry is erected. Moving somewhat more quickly through the Letter, we discover that the notion of pleasure has been transformed radically, and is, in fact, the fundamental criterion to which the doctrine of probable opinions appeals:

> Ponce et Sanchez sont de contraires avis; mais, parce qu'ils étaient tous deux savants, chacun rend son opinion probable. —Mais, mon Père, lui dis-je, on doit être bien bien embarrassé à choisir alors! Point du tout, dit-il, il n'y a qu'à suivre l'avis qui agrée le plus. (Letter 5, p. 79)

At the very end of the letter, however, Montalte, who has just turned to a sure tactic of *agrément* by having the Jesuit concoct the celebrated litany of cacaphonous casuist names, and who has just been promised further edification by the Jesuit, makes a parting reference to the upcoming happiness of the provincial recipient and all the other readers of the letters. "Je m'assure que vous en serez satisfait en attendant la suite." Pascal is sure that the content, the style, and the argumentation of the letter he has just finished will keep his readers occupied and satisfied until the next installment. The next five letters, in which the other fundamental doctrines of casuistic ethics and their scandalous consequences are examined, will follow the general lines of the collage set out in this fifth *Provinciale*.

At Letter 11, however, Pascal is obligated to veer onto another track, though not onto a different line. This new track runs parallel to the one taken in the previous five letters. This shift of focus, but not of aim, is occasioned by Jesuit responses that have become more sharply focused and smartly argued. It should be noted, however, that if Pascal is now in the position of having to defend his positions and his tactics, this does not necessarily mean that he is on the defensive. Indeed, the matter of factness with which he begins his first riposte to the Jesuit responses can suggest that he had been waiting for an occasion to direct his own assault against more fleshy targets, and to engage debate with an adversary whom he has been able to lure—"insensiblement"—out into the open, whom he has been able to goad out onto a battlefield that to all extents and purposes is the Jansenists' home terrain.[8] On this score, it might be recalled that in an earlier letter, Pascal has Montalte react sharply in the face of the Jesuit tactic of retreating into a mysterious and "eloquent" silence, once some local victory has been scored.[9] But now he has at his disposal something more than the Jesuit puppet he had confected out of stylistic necessity. He now can exploit as a useful part of his *matière brute* the sometimes clumsy, sometimes desperate, testimony of his adversaries. Their efforts will have moved them, just as Montalte had moved his overmatched adversary in Letters 5-10, into the snare laid out for them, a snare that fits squarely into the main line of his counter-fragmentational project.

Smarting from the success of the *petites lettres,* and feeling that their order had been intentionally misrepresented, the Jesuits have finally gotten around to serious counterattack. In reacting to these responses that accuse him of unfair editing, decontextualizing, and fragmenting, Pascal will engage in a discussion of his own tactics and strategy. As suggested earlier, this occasion can be to the advantage of the letter writer who will not want to miss the chance to highlight the propriety of his method. At the same time, he can reiterate and amplify the appropriateness of his stand by once again hanging the juicy maxims of the casuists out to dry in public. Moreover, if Pascal can show that his style, tone, and point of view are, in fact, perfectly adequate to the material being treated, he can further fragment the casuists' positions not only by showing them to be inherently defective, but also by exploiting his adversaries' public and publicized stubbornness in error. In short, just as he has been turning the casuist handbooks on morality and confessional politics against their proponents, he will also turn their objections to his method into a weapon that only seems to be defensive. This counteroffensive aspect is unmistakably clear in Letter 11 where the question of recourse to irony and sarcasm is taken up. At the same time as he makes his case for the fidelity of his quotation work, he ends up thematizing, justifying, and highlighting the whole citational project. His argument will want to deal with various aspects of his activity, the first of which being the matter of tone and style. He goes to some length, then, in justifying the use to which he puts the quotations lifted from Jesuit sources, as well as the tone in which he (ab)uses them.

The first point he makes derives from an inference on the part of the Jesuits that it is they who take the high road with regard to things sacred. From this lofty perspective they level accusations against the author of the *Lettres* not so much for reporting their teachings, but for glossing those teachings with an irony that they link to blasphemy:

> ...l'un des principaux points de votre défense est que je n'ai pas parlé sérieusement de vos maximes: c'est ce que vous répétez dans tous vos écrits, et que vous poussez jusqu'à dire *Que j'ai tourné les choses saintes en raillerie.* (Letter 11, p. 148)

In his turn, Pascal responds by targeting two features of the Jesuit riposte: it is, he says, one thing to complain that the casuist maxims are not treated with sufficient seriousness—throughout the letters he will operate on the assumption that while the maxims themselves can hardly be taken seriously, their threat and consequences are indeed serious—it is quite another to consider them as sacred. In his view, the distinction between genuinely sacred language and the sort of mutation espoused by the Jesuits would be so great that, just as it would be impious to lack respect for the former, it would be an even greater impiety to lack disrespect for the latter. Following this logic, Pascal will go on to juxtapose the "divine beauty" and "holy majesty" that renders the truths of Christianity worthy of love and veneration with the impiety and impertinence that render false positions horrible and ridiculous. Pascal insists on the correlation of love and fear in the service of truth and of hatred and scorn in the face of error. It is faithfulness to these positions that compel the saints to "repousser avec force la malice des impies et à confondre avec risée leur égarement et leur folie" (Letter 11, p. 149).

The force Pascal invests, and wants his readers to invest, in the mocking attitudes of the saints is critical to the patina he wants to give his own irony. First, the *risée* of the saints is cited as a method of confusing or confounding the impious in their *égarement* and *folie*. It would not only point to a result (confusion of the impious) but also suggests the means to attain that result—also confusion. The strayings of the Church's adversaries would not only be cited, but would be fused together in that collective, choral laughter (*risée*) to highlight the basic inconsistency (*confusion*) and distance (*égarements*) from orthodox traditions and values. A second consideration comes with Pascal's reiteration of the expression *haine et mépris*. In effect, this expression, which, in its first use, refers to the saints' reaction to the errors against the Church, picks up significant strength in the second usage: "Car ne voyons-nous pas que Dieu hait et méprise les pécheurs tout ensemble." Pascal does not hesitate to ally himself with the most powerful forces he can legitimately muster. His own tactic of scorn and of confusing are already authorized by antecedents of the most terrifying sort; and it is not by chance that he turns to the rhetoric of terror by localizing the scornful, derisive aspect of *la sagesse divine* at the moment of death.[10] This divine wisdom, the *logos*—the word denotes not only the truths contained in authentic sacred texts, but God himself—is said to join forces with vengeance and furor. Man's *folie*, as manifested by aberrant thinking of which the Jesuits have provided the model, will be submitted to divine *fureur*. This conjunction of forces will also be enhanced by *la moquerie et la risée* as the sinner is condemned to eternal torture. And the saints, taking their cue from God, will amplify this last laugh by "trembling and laughing" in the face of the condemned sinners. Pascal's evocation of this macabre chorus of laughers recalls and, to a certain extent, responds to, the chorus of Dominicans assenting to the oppressive Molinist terminology in Letter 2.

With this terrible eschatology as textual backdrop and theological guarantor, Pascal's own *raillerie* is valorized and at the same time rhetorically attenuated. His mocking of the casuist wisdom, while part of a long and divinely sanctioned tradition, is of relatively little might when compared to the threat this tradition actually holds. Pascal situates his own discourse in an even larger one that provides him with a reserve of precedents and quotations; namely from David, from Job and from God himself. Indeed, God's ironic treatment of Adam would not only justify Pascal's own tactics, but would also serve as an example befitting the basic theological positions percolating just below the surface of the assault on the casuists' moral politics. God's derisive jab at Adam—"voilà l'homme qui est devenu comme l'un de nous"—expresses not only the sin, but its consequences, the ironic dismissal of the sinner. To usurp divine prerogative is to incur irony as well as ire: "Dieu, en punition, rendit [Adam] sujet à la mort, et qu'après l'avoir réduit à cette misérable condition qui était due à son péché, il se moque de lui en cet état par ces paroles de risée: voilà l'homme..." The evocation of Adam's incursion into God's dominion works as a strong image of what Molinist theology is about: despite his radical fall from grace, man would dare to make himself master of his own fortunes for salvation. And on the level of morality, this same fallen creature would boldly set himself up, as in the case of the casuist Bauny, as he, who by force of logic, natural reason, and magic formulae would take away the sins of the world.

In Pascal's text, the scriptural language leveled at Adam serves as authorization for further quotes in support of that position. The quotes from St. John Chrysostom and other authoritative figures, underscoring the appropriate use of irony and sarcasm, are, of course, designed to provide Pascal with powerful allies and powerful precedent—a tactic he continues in the succeeding paragraphs where the prophets, Saint Augustine, Saint Jérôme, Saint Bernard, and the Fathers of the Church are all enlisted to the cause. In evoking these partisans of an irony put surgically to the service of sacred values, Pascal effectively situates himself as part of an unbroken line of authentic and enlightened champions.

He concludes his justification of the use of irony by invoking an expert witness in such matters, the third-century apologist, Tertullian. From Tertullian's polemic against the Valentinian heretics—or more precisely from Arnauld's appropriation of that work—Pascal gleens the following:

> Ce que j'ai fait n'est qu'un jeu avant un véritable combat. J'ai plutôt montré les blessures qu'on vous peut faire que je ne vous en ai fait. Que s'il se trouve des endroits où l'on soit excité à rire, c'est parce que les sujets mêmes y portaient. Il y a beaucoup de choses qui méritent d'être moquées et jouées de la sorte, de peur de leur donner du poids en les combattant sérieusement. Rien n'est plus dû à la vanité que la risée; et c'est proprement à la vérité à qui il appartient à rire, parce qu'elle est gaie, et de se jouer de ses ennemis, parce qu'elle est assurée de la victoire. Il est vrai qu'il faut prendre garde que les railleries ne soient pas basses et indignes de la vérité. Mais à cela près, quand on pourra s'en servir avec adresse, c'est un devoir que d'en user. (p. 151)

To these "*excellente paroles*," Pascal adds some excellent words of his own:

> Ne trouvez-vous pas, mes Pères, que ce passage est bien juste à notre sujet? Les lettres que j'ai faites jusqu'ici ne sont qu'un jeu avant un véritable combat. Je n'ai fait encore que me jouer, et vous montrer plutôt les blessures qu'on vous peut faire que je ne vous en ai fait. J'ai exposé simplement vos passages sans y faire presque de réflexion. Que si on y a été excité à rire, c'est parce que les sujets y portaient d'eux-mêmes. (p. 151)

In considering the role Tertullian's text plays in Pascal's methodology and his argument in favor of that methodology, it will be helpful to approach that text from three intersecting angles: 1) the fundamental notions introduced in the original argument; 2) the slight but significant variants Pascal introduces in his translation of the text and 3) his exploitation or rewriting of the text. Attention to these three versions gives us a working sense of Pascal's *main à la pâte*. With regard to the fundamental notions that appear in the three versions of the text, there is one that appears consistently, namely, the idea of the game. Recourse to irony and mockery is characterized as amusement, as a light-handed prelude to the real struggle that such recourse only announces. This is underscored further by the suggestion that the "game" both Tertullian and Pascal play is, at bottom, a warning, one that serves to envelop their activity in the cloak of fair play. Their activity is to show what danger their adversaries risk to themselves in pursuing policies exposed at earlier points in the arguments of the two polemicists. That, at least, is the impression Pascal wants to give. It is in his interest to convince his readers that he has found a classical quotation—from a recognized champion against heresy no less—custom-made for his own designs. What Tertullian actually said was, however, somewhat different. Here with my highlighting is Arnauld's "very exact" translation of the Latin:[11] Ce que je *m'en vais faire* n'est qu'un jeu et une escarmouche avant un juste combat. Je *me contenterai de les effleurer*, et de leur montrer plutôt les blessures qu'on peut faire, que je ne leur en ferai de véritables." In the main, the two versions are quite similar. It should be noted, however, that Pascal has edited out the notion of the skirmish (*escarmouche*) and, with it, some of the sabre rattling of the original text, as well as the verb *effleurer* (to brush lightly against). He has also changed Tertullian's future tenses to the present perfect, a move effectively transforming a modality of intent in the original text into a *fait accompli* in the translation. Now, while insistence on these fragile shifts may seem at first to be precious and hairsplitting, they do invite a closer look at the licence Pascal permits himself, a license that fairly well indexes his rhetorical tactics.

The shifting of verb tenses allows him to give the impression that he and Tertullian are on precisely the same tactical and ideological wavelength. A cause held in common would authorize him to appropriate and recast an antecedent text to his own needs. This affords him the possibility of a convenient reinscription of a translated text passing for a perfect rendering of the original into the flow of his own argument. To wit: the variant translation "ce que j'ai fait n'est qu'un jeu" slides seamlessly into "les lettres que j'ai faites jusqu'ici ne sont qu'un jeu." This gives the impression that the *véritable combat* is about to come—in letters where he will set to the business of defending the "playful" ones already in circulation. Basically what he seems to be saying is this: if you want to take the gloves off, I'll oblige, but you are really asking for it this time. The requoting of Tertullian is momentarily broken, or rather, amended, to reiterate the point—and with it the implied menace—of the main event yet to come. "Je n'ai fait encore que me jouer." He then picks up the thread of the quote from Tertullian: "et vous montrer plutôt les blessures qu'on peut faire que je ne vous en ai fait." The quote is again interrupted in a way that yields gracefully and naturally to Pascal's own discursive flow: "J'ai exposé simplement vos passages sans y faire presque de réflexion." This would then further define the nature of the game. In effect, Pascal wants his readers, be they friendly or hostile, to consider his first pass through Jesuit moral theology and confessional politics as little more than a sampling. To this point he would have only provided something of a scrap book of his adversaries' precepts. Indeed, in Letter 7 he has already claimed that all he has done is to report "simplement" and quote "fidèlement" the original casuistic texts.[12] It is suggested that on the second pass, however, those scraps are to be enhanced by a more critical modality (*réflexion*). Tertullian's wisdom and Pascal's appropriation of it are in this same paragraph put in direct contextual touch with what is then to pass for the wisdom of the casuists. Typically Pascal picks an item that unmistakably underscores the outrageousness of the quantitative thinking with which his reader has become familiar.[13] The juxtaposition of the casuistic language with the "serious" texts of Tertullian and Pascal makes it come across as even more silly than it might have been in the context of the handbooks from which it had been gleaned.

A second point made in defense of the citational tactics of the middle letters is one Pascal has to develop in far less detail, since it is hardly the kind of issue upon which theoretical considerations need be brought to bear. The Jesuit complaint is that Pascal has gone over ground that other critics have also found objectionable. According to this logic, his work would be tainted by redundancy. To this Pascal has only to respond that the objectionable material is still circulating, and that no effort has been made to suppress, disown, or amend it. And in light of this persistence, it is still incumbent on those who battle under the banner of truth to continue their campaign.

Pascal's response to these two objections—that he has turned supposedly sacred texts into parodic mutations, and that he has simply opened up closet doors on skeletons whose bones he took efforts to dig up in the first place—is energized by a strong dose of common sense. Indeed, while the terrain upon which he struggles is not precisely the same as it was in the early letters, and while the tone may have changed with the choice of terrain, the person arguing the Jansenists' cause in the later letters is not radically different from the picaresque hero of the early ones. Montalte still speaks the voice of common sense, and his argument against the excesses of casuistry are the arguments used against any excess. It is based on restraint, order, and logic—buzzwords of a classical ideal. His is the argument, if not of any *honnête homme*, at least of an *honnête homme croyant*, who, for all his faith, has not lost touch with the discourse of the world when that discourse is not at basic odds with the demands of faith. This is underscored in the same Letter 11 when, still in defense of his "secular" approach to the casuist texts, Pascal loudly raises this counter objection:

> Quoi! faut-il employer la force de l'Ecriture et de la tradition pour montrer que c'est tuer son ennemi en trahison que de lui donner des coups d'épée par derrière, et dans une embuche, et que c'est acheter un bénéfice que de donner de l'argent comme motif pour se le faire résigner?

What he is getting at here, by refusing to turn to scripture on such matters, is to put his own text squarely in the current of common understanding and common sense, which in matters of morality have to be consonant with God's law. The language he uses, the positions expressed in that language, and the moral codes supported in it are commonsensical, they are what is known from experience and what is known in the heart to be true. Many of the issues at stake in the tussle over morality need not be cast in a metaphysical light. The real world and the language of that world are sufficient to define for us what an ambush is, what treachery is, what simony is, what a duel is. The concepts are coextensive with the language we commonly use to talk about and define them. And the language the Jesuits use, because it is used in ways that are divisive and deflective, because it falsifies theological concepts and moral codes, must, by necessity, take on the status of an *issue* in the Jansenist argument.

Pascal will not allow his own use of that same language to bear down on the substantive points of his argument. He refuses to be pulled into a protracted technical discussion of his quotation work. His refusal to cross swords with the Jesuits on this issue is not motivated by fear of being found unfair in his use of Jesuit texts—scholarly investigation has judged him sufficiently faithful to his sources—but because such discussion would reduce him to dealing with what he deems ancillary matters.

> Si je n'avais qu'à répondre aux trois impostures qui restent sur
> l'homicide, je n'aurais pas besoin d'un long discours, et vous les verrez
> ici réfutées en peu de mots: mais comme je trouve bien plus important
> de donner au mode de l'horreur de vos opinions sur ce sujet que de
> justifier la fidélité de mes citations, je serai obligé d'employer la plus
> grande partie de cette lettre à la réfutation de vos maximes [...].
> (Letter 14, p. 187)

Because, in Pascal's view, the Jesuits have corrupted language in order to corrupt the concepts and codes of morality, his text will be relentless in pushing the notion that the Jesuit works themselves represent fundamental misuses of language, and that those misuses are not isolated occurrences. The Jesuit responses to the earlier letters on morality provide Pascal with a supplementary impetus to exploit the notion of a system at work. These responses, in which Jesuit damage control experts attempt to justify the order and its logic, serve as a pretext for further analytical reading, that is, the kind of reading that will break the system down; that will fragment it by showing it to be an incoherent jumble governed, nonetheless, by the underlying principle of probabalism and sanctioned by the order's imprimatur. Pascal's reading, his ana-lysis (the greek term carries two resonances: decomposition and resolution) is designed precisely to effect this breaking down. And in that objective, Jesuitism has to be convicted of actually constituting a system. Pascal gives precious little evidence of being preoccupied specifically and intently on the demise of the Jesuit order. His persistence seems, rather, to be linked directly to his sense of the Church, to its past and its future.

To this end, the *Provinciales* serve to provide something like the composite portrait used by modern day detectives. These portraits, gener ated either by the testimony of several witnesses, each adding details and features to a mysterious face, or by a single witness who chooses from a reserve of stock features to generate the face which is then submitted to public view and scrutiny. It is true that the face drawn from such composing may not be a perfect likeness of the suspect; but it very well may be faithful enough to bring about the sought-after indictment. Such appears to be the case in the *Provinciales,* where even if each and every quotation has not been rendered with absolute accuracy, or with all its contextual baggage, the suspect, in this case excessive casuistry, seems to have been drawn with enough detail and resemblance to justify the charges brought against it.

In Letter 13, Pascal punctuates the seriousness and validity of his citational strategy by underscoring the disingenuousness with which the Jesuits handle the very material he appropriates from them. Indeed, he will designate their shiftiness as one of the most "subtle" aspects of their political prowess (Letter 13, p. 183). Pascal's adjective points not only to the finesse and cleverness of his adversaries' tactics, but also to their general imperceptibility. To be subtle is to want to pass unnoticed. It is, of course, very much to the point of the enterprise, whose collective title is the *Lettres provinciales,* to bring imperceptible practice very much to public perception; which is precisely what Pascal is about when he brings to the attention of his readers the subtlety of the Jesuit tactic of separating in their writings the maxims that they conjoin in their opinions (*avis*). The result of this disjunction is that pronouncements and prescriptions, which in isolation would be either outrageous or innocuous, become dangerous in the extreme when linked to a principle that does not appear in the same context. Pascal offers the following example: in one place it might be declared that "plusieurs théologiens sont d'avis qu'on peut tuer pour un soufflet." As it stands the statement is nothing more than a *question de fait.* The fact expressed in the statement might be scandalous, but it is all the same nothing more than *un simple récit,* a report. When conjoined with the principle of probabilism, which says that whatever supposedly serious theologians approve of may be considered probable, and therefore certain, the simple *récit* is transformed into a highly dangerous legalization. In this regard, Pascal considers as part of his own corrective enterprise a rhetorical strategy designed on the one hand to "joindre ensemble [...] principes et [...] maximes" (p. 184) and on the other to "rassembler ces maximes" that the Jesuits separate in efforts to justify themselves. This strategy will not only allow him to indict the unsavory positions of his adversaries, but also to point once again to the chaos and confusion bubbling just below the surface of the casuists' teachings. In basic contrast to the uniformity of truth, it is this "mélange confus de toutes sortes d'opinions" that renders the *system* of casuistry so suspect and intolerable. "C'est donc cette variété qui vous confond davantage. L'uniformité serait plus supportable" (Letter 13, p. 185).

The textual tactics of the Jesuit responses consist in dispersal, fragmentation, and separation. Speculation is judiciously kept away from practice; maxims are parsed out and kept at a distance from each other in a variety of written works; disclaimer and condemnation of particular errors are put to paper and there made to appear applicable to a completely different issue. Pascal's task is to bring this separation to bear as part of the thing he combats and as part of his citational strategy. His conjunctive activities are put to the service of readers who might otherwise be blinded by what appears to be the protestations by the Jesuit respondants that homicidal revenge in the face of a slap, for example, is condemned by the casuists Vasquez and Suarez. For his part, Pascal argues for a clear view based on a counterapplication of the doctrine of probable opinions, that is, of the overriding (or underpinning) principle serving as the glue that holds the mishmash of casuist pronouncements together. Principle, which in the unequivocal language to which Pascal subscribes, is given general precedence over relative, often contradictory individual cases, is exploited in a way that defines and thereby generalizes specific protestations and denials.

> Vous dites donc ici que Vasquez ne souffre point les meurtres. Mais que dites-vous d'un autre côté, mes Pères? Que la probabilité d'un sentiment n'empêche pas la probabilité du sentiment contraire? Et en un autre lieu, qu'il est permis de suivre l'opinion la moins probable et la plus sûre. (Letter 13, p. 184)

To Pascal's way of thinking, the procedural and textual gap has only to be closed to effect a powerful and persuasive rebuke both to the casuist project and to the maneuvering in the Jesuit response to the *Provinciales*.

The responses tendered by his outraged adversaries would, for the author of the letters, be completely coherent with the specious logic already characterizing Jesuitism. This logic, put forth as disinculpation, is in fact a diversionary tactic designed to blind those who do not really know what they are looking at. "Ces témoignages, séparés du reste de votre doctrine, pourraient éblouir ceux qui ne l'entendent pas assez." Pascal is, of course, prepared to make the textual synapse conjoining principle and practice: "Mais il faut joindre ensemble vos principes et vos maximes" (Letter 13, p. 184). In so doing, the fruit that the Jesuits had hoped to obtain is said to wither and disappear. Indeed, it will have already been poisoned by their own doctors. Pascal merely puts it on the table: "Que devient donc, mes Pères, le fruit que vous espériez de toutes ces citations? Il disparait, puisqu'il ne faut, pour votre condamnation, que rassembler ces maximes que vous séparez pour votre justification" (Letter 13, p. 185).

As this fruit, this discursive sustenance that the Jesuits had hoped to gain in their own citational strategies, disappears under the weight of an assemblage of quotations, the basic chaos of their positions becomes all the more apparent. The casuists cited by Nouet and Annat in their rebuttal, and called upon to prove that the Jesuits maintain the very opposite of the accusations leveled by Pascal, end up ricocheting against the Society and the ideology they are supposed to rescue. Moreover, they provide an active illustration of the main points Pascal wants to make in his own quotation and collage work. They underscore the disorder consequent to one of the main features of casuistry, namely, its extension. His task has been to promote the notion that the excessive casuistry to which his adversaries subscribe is already locked in the prison of its own device, and that its extensive nature, its promise to reconcile a multiplicity of often contradictory cases, dooms it to logical self-destruction. To this end, Pascal produces a dizzying mix of positions and counter-positions. For example, Lessius would justify those who want to kill; Vasquez those who do not; and if the former speaks as a pagan with regard to homicide, he speaks as a good Christian with regard to almsgiving; and Vasquez the opposite on both; and the two will in all cases be right, even if they know themselves to be wrong. Subscription to the underlying doctrine of probable opinions requires deference to positions that each would judge condemnable in conscience. "C'est donc cette variété qui vous confond davantage. L'uniformité serait plus supportable" (Letter 13, p. 185).

Pascal's observation is a rich one. The variety, that is the flexibility, of the Jesuit system—and the attempted defense of that system—are said to confound the Jesuits further. In addition to first confusions—Molinism itself and its projection into casuistry—the very principle that would hold it all together, that would give it all an internal coherence, will actually engender further confusion, precisely by fusing together fundamentally incompatible positions, positions that Pascal wants his reader to apprehend simultaneously as not only confounding to the system of casuistry itself but also to the principles of the Jesuit order as articulated by Ignatius Loyola and the first generals of the Society. In this view, nothing would be as foreign to these venerable figures as the *mélange confus* that has since come to dominate the thinking of the Society. In this way, he effects a fragmentation that isolates the casuistry of the "evolved" Jesuits from the more honorable designs of their predecessors and thus gives implicit preference to earlier visions of the Church and its mission. Pointing out that he has more important concerns, Pascal demurs on this point. He prefers to engrave in his reader's mind the notion that the Jesuits, as presently constitued, are in fact *déchus*,[14] a term that carries some resonances of the larger first fall from grace, the consequences of which the Molinism adopted by the Jesuits wants to minimize.

The *mélange confus,* this confused assemblage already in place, which becomes the assembling or fusing of maxims in the *Provinciales*, is, for all its (self)righteousness and muscle, supposed to reflect a spirit of charity. In Letter 11, where he delimits the rules for determining whether judgments and recriminations are in the tradition set down by the Church Fathers, Pascal declares himself governed by a principle of discretion. According to this principle, the cuts he makes would be those of a surgeon, not the indiscriminate hacking and slashing of someone outraged and out of control. The surgical, well-intentioned motivation for his cutting and pasting has kept him from reporting everything he might have:

> Vous savez bien, mes Pères, que je n'ai pas rapporté, des maximes de vos auteurs, celles qui vous auraient été les plus sensibles, quoique j'eusse pu le faire, et même sans pécher contre la discrétion, non plus que de savants hommes et très catholiques, mes Pères, qui l'on fait autrefois; et tous ceux qui ont lu vos auteurs savent aussi bien que vous combien en cela je vous ai épargnés: outre que je n'ai parlé en aucune sorte contre ce qui vous regarde chacun en particulier; et je serais faché d'avoir rien dit des fautes secrètes et personnelles, quelque preuve que j'en eusse. Car je sais que c'est le propre de la haine et de l'animosité, et qu'on ne doit jamais le faire, à moins qu'il y ait une nécessité bien pressante pour le bien de l'Eglise. (Letter 11, p. 155)

This deference to discretion would, in fact, be part of a larger context of charity, itself reflective of an urge to convert his adversary. And once again, more like the surgeon, Pascal sees himself deriving a salutary medication for his adversaries, a bitter and embittering pill that is supposed to do wonders for the system, by bringing the purveyors of casuistic excess back to their senses, back to the larger sense of reasonableness marking the Church and her teaching. "Je me sens obligé de vous procurer cette *confusion salutaire* dont parle l'Ecriture, qui est presque l'unique remède" (Letter 16, p. 217). This salvific confusion that Pascal would procure for, and at the expense of, his adversaries shows two faces. The first, or general one, is already circulating in the form of the ten letters in which Pascal fuses maxims from various sources to form a dynamic indictment of casuistic thinking. The second face of the salvific confusion is linked to

Pascal's own identity, to the exploitation of his own mysteriousness, his autonomy, and his otherness.

Periodically, Pascal will take pains to underscore his own elusiveness. In Letter 8, for example, his tone is very much thumb to nose:

> Vous ne penseriez pas que personne eût la curiosité de savoir qui nous sommes; cependant il y a des gens qui essayent de le deviner, mais il rencontrent mal. Les uns me prennent pour un docteur de Sorbonne: Les autres attribuent mes lettres à quatre ou cinq personnes, qui, comme moi, ne sont ni prêtres ni ecclésiastiques. Tous ces faux soupçons me font connaître que je n'ai pas mal réussi dans le dessein que j'ai de n'être connu que de vous, et du bon Père qui souffre toujours mes visites, et dont je souffre toujours les discours, quoique avec peine. (Letter 8, p. 109)

In Letter 16, his treatment of the subject becomes harsher and more aggressive. The point he feels obliged to hammer home is that he is not of Port-Royal. An important clause of the Jesuit defense against the attacks buffeting them is that they are the work of just another deranged soul from Port-Royal, of yet another member of a communion of heretics; for in the Jesuit logic, all opposition must go by the name of Port-Royal, and Port-Royal is heretical.

Pascal's intention is then to fragment the opposition forces of which he is a part by establishing himself and, it is implied, others, as independent sources of trouble for the Jesuits: "Dieu n'a pas renfermé dans ce nombre seul tous ceux qu'il veut opposer à vos désordres" (Letter 16, p. 217). Later, in Letter 17, Pascal speaks most forcefully, even provocatively, of the difference between his own solitary project and the corporative errors, truculence, and resistance of the Jesuits. In this letter, it is, on the one hand, a question of disputing the contention that anyone opposing the Society of Jesus is, in fact, "one person," and that this person is effectively, automatically, and always deviant; and on the other, of promoting the notion that the Jesuits constitute a single body and that the aberrant, exaggerated uses to which the science of casuistry is being put are imputable to that body:

> Je vous admire, mon Père, de considérer ainsi tous ceux qui vous sont contraires comme une seule personne. Votre haine les embrasse tous ensemble, et en forme comme un corps de réprouvés, dont vous voulez

que chacun réponde pour tous les autres. Il y a bien de la différence
entre les Jésuites et ceux qui les combattent. Vous composez véritablement un corps sous un seul chef. (Letter 17, pp. 236-37)

And if the Jesuits do in fact constitute a single body, their teachings,
needing the approval of the head of the body, are given *de facto* official
status.

On the other hand, by arguing that the opponents of Jesuitism and
the excessive casuistry characteristic of it do not in fact form a single body,
and thereby inferring that opposition comes from a multiplicity of autonomous camps, he is to a certain extent liberating his letters from blanket
condemnation. In a famous and controversial section of this same Letter
17, Pascal taunts his Jesuit adversaries when he reminds them of something
of which they can be only painfully aware: that they are the victims of a
"main invisible." Moreover this hand does not belong to the identifiable
body (Port-Royal) against which they direct their attack. Not only would he
be detached from that body, he declares himself also detached from the
world. He is "sans engagement, sans attachement, sans liaison, sans
relations, sans affaires." By presenting himself as this disembodied
opposition to everything the Jesuit moral codes and theology would
represent for him, he is defusing the potential damage of the Jesuit
response, which must continue to shoot in the dark, in many directions. He
is but a hand out in the darkness, an invisible hand that busies itself by
leafing through manuals to engage in a double fragmentation: first by
cutting up the manuals and pasting them back together; and secondly, by
unleashing this new version of the Jesuit texts so as to publicize the
confusion inherent in the relativistic moral system they champion. The
writer of the letters will exploit his advantage as an autonomous and
anonymous force in order to procure a *confusion salutaire* for his adversaries. The Jesuits will not know exactly where to strike, since their most
obvious target, Port-Royal, would, in this pronouncement, have been
moved out of range. So Pascal keeps himself hidden to snipe away at the
Jesuits as he defuses the attacks against Port-Royal.

One of the most virulent Jesuit attacks against Port-Royal would
want to establish an ideological association with Calvinist heresy. This
association, based ostensibly on the question of real presence in the
Eucharist, would itself derive from purported denials of this presence by
Port-Royal. Pascal ups the rhetorical ante quickly to propose that such

collusion with Geneva would necessarily entail holding the Eucharist in abomination. Having established that the Jesuit attack against Port-Royal is based on this point, Pascal can buffet his adversaries with the very term purportedly held in such blasphemous esteem by the Jansenists:

> Car, dites-moi, mes Pères, si ces religieuses et leurs directeurs étaient d'intelligence avec Genève contre le très Saint-Sacrement de l'Autel, ce qui est horrible à penser, pourquoi auraient-elles pris pour le principal objet de leur piété ce sacrement qu'elles auraient en abomination? Pouquoi auraient-elles joint à leur règle l'institution du Saint-Sacrement? Pourquoi auraient-elles pris l'habit du Saint-Sacrement, appelé leur église l'Eglise du Saint-Sacrement? Pouquoi auraient-elles demandé et obtenu de Rome la confirmation de cette institution, et le pouvoir de dire tous les jeudis l'office du Saint-Sacrement [...]. (Letter 16, pp. 218-19)

This rhetorical pummeling, in which the term "Saint-Sacrement" is used in a way that recalls, if only contrapuntally, the Molinists' own magic word, is significant not only in terms of the specific theological cause it represents, but also in terms of the larger polemical objectives of the *Provinciales*. One of those objectives, laid out in the declaration of intention leading directly to this refutation of the charge that the nuns at Port-Royal are in cahoots with Geneva, is to move the Jesuit accusers to a sense of horror of themselves and the evil they do. "Ce que j'en dirai ici ne sera pas pour montrer leur innocence, mais pour montrer votre malice. Je veux seulement vous en faire horreur à vous-mêmes" (Letter 16, p. 216). Once again, Pascal is not to content himself with righteous and perfunctory finger waggling. His rhetorical and editorial strategy, especially in the middle and late letters has been to lead the Jesuits into the mire of their own texts in order to bring them to a recognition of the monstrous quality of their moral codes and the applications that derive from them. As part of his case against the slanderous and malicious accusations of the Jesuits, Pascal produces an impressive series of textual references gleaned from Jansenist sources underscoring the orthodoxy of Port-Royal's positions with regard to the Eucharist. Now, while his evidence appears to be altogether convincing, and while it does, as he asserts, clearly show the *grande impudence* of the Jesuit accusation, Pascal determines that it alone will not be sufficient to the larger designs of his polemic. He insists upon twisting the Jesuits back upon themselves: "je veux encore vous faire prononcer cet arrêt à vous-mêmes contre vous-mêmes" (Letter 16, p. 220).

To this effect, he extracts from the work of the Jesuit Meynier a proclamation asserting that if M. Arnauld maintained that in the consecrated bread there no longer was bread, but rather the body of Jesus Christ, he, Meynier, would consider Arnauld "entièrement contre Genève." Such is, of course, Arnauld's stated position on the matter. Hence the Jesuit campaign against Arnauld and through him, Port-Royal, would stand accused, indeed pronounced guilty, of bad faith, idle propositions, or simple calumny. Pascal's intention is to have his Jesuit readers find in the folds of their own overextended discourse the contradictions that generate not only a sense and a sentence of guilt against themselves, but also a sense of horror, that is, a sense of having pushed things beyond the limits of sanity, of having created a monster that turns to devour its maker. In Pascal's view, the Jesuits have in fact gone so far that any other outrage could only be less surprising and offensive. "Je veux faire entendre à tout le monde qu'après cela il n'y a rien dont vous ne soyez capable" (Letter 16, p. 216). Pascal's insistence on the calumnious activities of the Jesuits extends then beyond the parameters that a defense of his compatriots, or even of his own rhetorical strategies, would naturally establish. Calumny or lying, if proven, effectively banishes its purveyor from the privileges of credibility. The liar's words reflect, indeed they become the flesh of sinister intentions. "Je ferai voir que votre intention est de mentir et de calomnier" (Letter 15, p. 202). The privilege given this issue is underscored by its predominance in the last letters addressed to the Jesuits directly.

Towards the end of Letter 16, Pascal submits his adversaries to an especially devastating crossfire by once again training their own maxims against them, by cutting and collating their books in such a way that their pages are, to speak figuratively, carried off in the wind. Moreover, he credits the auto-destructive aspect to divine intervention, itself bearing less on Pascal's own project than on the initial formulation of the Jesuit texts. Pascal's work would be that of a scholar, of an agent whose erudition and application have been put to the task of finding the "truth" inscribed by God himself in the labyrinth of lies, exaggerations, and aberrations marking the casuist texts: "Certainement, mes Pères, vous seriez capables de produire par là beaucoup de maux, si Dieu n'avait permis que vous ayez fourni vous-mêmes les moyens de les empêcher et de rendre toutes vos impostures sans effet [...]" (Letter 16, p. 231). As agent, he has only to publish the strange maxim designed to excuse calumny in order to destroy any claims to credibility. His argument, brilliant in its simplicity and inescapable in its application, is as follows. The false position carried in the calumny can be effective only if backed by an unimpeachable reputation for truthfulness: "Un médisant ne peut réussir, s'il n'est en estime d'abhorrer la médisance comme un crime dont il est incapable" (Letter 16, p. 231). Now, since the Jesuits have already put into writing and into practice the principle that would authorize slander and lying, any advantage they might have hoped to realize in slandering the Jansenists is lost in the deliberate, if ill-conceived, relinquishing of claims to sincerity. The deployment of a general principle condoning and legitimizing the dissemination of falsehood is made to rebound against subsequent protestations of sincerity the Jesuits might be inclined to make. The principle, designed to override the culpability normally attached to such malfeasance is made to ricochet in such a way as to destroy its own usefulness. Such would be the natural bent of evil: "tant le mal est contraire à soi-même, et tant il s'embarrasse et se détruit par sa propre malice" (Letter 16, p. 231).

What Pascal has done is to situate Jesuit thinking in a circuit of evil, not just by declaring it such, but by demonstrating it to be so. He has shown that the Jesuits have run the risk of losing everything and gaining nothing in opting to be forthright on the subject of their calumnious tactics. The ingenuousness of "putting their confidence" in lies will, in the argument Pascal promotes, end up in nothing less than a fulfillment of scriptural wisdom:

> Votre ruine sera semblable à celle d'une haute muraille qui tombe d'une chute imprévue, et à celle d'un vaisseau de terre qu'on brise et qu'on écrase en toutes ses parties par un effort si puissant et si universel qu'il n'en restera pas un test avec lequel on puisse puiser en peu d'eau ou prêter un peu de feu. (Letter 16, p. 232)

The counter-fragmentational intent of Pascal's argument is underscored clearly in this passage. Lies and deception which, for Pascal, stand as natural extensions of the edifice of casuistry in large part built and occupied by the Jesuits, will bring the walls of that edifice tumbling down. Falling from a great height, the walls will fragment into pieces of stone and mortar—these pieces, these maxims, formulas, prescriptions, and circumlocutions will be splayed about in the disorder inherent in the apparent order and "reasonableness" of the casuistic structure.

A second image in the scriptural text appropriated by Pascal, that of the shattered earthen vessel, is perhaps even more germane to Pascal's counter-fragmentational maneuverings. This vessel—and it may be of more than incidental interest that it is made of earth, as it parallels the earthly (and sometimes earthy) constituants of the casuist moral prescriptions) will, it is predicted, break and shatter into "all its parts." The effort characterized not only as forceful (*si puissant*) but also as *universel,* is to bear with unrelenting pressure on the vase, this object designed to hold life sustaining water or the flame of wisdom. The pressure, triggered from the outside by the kind of archaeological probing and structuring in which Pascal engages, will eventually come from the inside, from significant contradictions such as the frank and "truthful" adherence to untruth. The explosion of the system is to be so thorough that, if we be permitted to take the prophet's image (and Pascal's inscription of it in his attack) literally, the argument of casuistry will no longer hold water ("il n'en restera pas un test avec lequel on puisse puiser un peu d'eau").

The contradiction Pascal exposes in the casuist texts, as well as the kind of questions he poses (so simple that they cannot be side-stepped by appeal to the *distinguo*[15] or to the obscurantist language of scholasticism) are intended to bring the Jesuits and their supporters to the silence of a dead end. The system of casuistry, turned against itself, will, in the end, shut itself down. The most trenchant example of this inherently contradictory mechanism, of this circuit that will inevitably short out, appears in Letter 12: "Oseriez-vous le traiter de simoniaque dans vos confessionaux, quelque sentiment que vous en ayez par vous-mêmes, puisqu'il *aurait droit de vous fermer la bouche, ayant agi selon l'avis de tant de docteurs graves?"* (p. 169). This case of the confessor caught up in the prison of his own device is a model of the more general dead end towards which Pascal sees casuistry leading, and towards which he is more than willing to prod his adversaries. The dead end of maxims, prescriptions, and pronouncements, principles and practices that "*s'entredétruisent,*" as do the responses of the Jesuits to the letters buffeting them,[16] would establish the environment of silence in which the language of truth might be properly heard and received.

Chapter 4

The Motifs of Truth and Truthfulness

IT CAN BE ARGUED THAT PASCAL'S fundamental concern in the *Provinciales* is neither grace nor morals, neither Arnauld nor Annat, neither Jansenism nor Jesuitism. While matters such as these are obviously basic to the sense of his polemic, they are more appropriately considered as variants on a single theme: truth. It is against the touchstone of truth that these and other questions raised in the *Provinciales* are to be tested, verified, and defined. Truth, always a slippery beast, is never so slippery as when questions of religion are at stake. One group's truth may very well be another's heresy. It is clear that the Jesuits were as revolted by the Jansenists as the Jansenists with them. It is equally certain that each side saw itself as being right. Henri Lefebvre parses things along these lines: "Aux Jansénistes, l'essence, le noyau dogmatique et abstrait, aux Jésuites, le réalisme politique, le sens du monde réel social, la raison empiriquement pratique."[1] From this perspective it may be possible to argue that Pascal and his associates willfully skew things in their favor, that is, in favor of principles out of step with human shortcomings; and that the rhetorical campaign known as the *Lettres provinciales* is at bottom a clever hatchet job undertaken to embarrass a despised enemy and promote the political fortunes, as well as the theological stock, of a particularly strident minority group. On the other hand, it could be argued that the Jansenists were right; that their vision of the Church and its tradition was a fundamentally sound and worthy one that *obligated* them to pursue an adversary whom they perceived as posing an evident threat to traditions and precedents cherished as truth itself is cherished.

Whether or not the Pascal of the *Provinciales* was right or wrong, whether he was a champion of truth or a wily, willful manipulator of circumstances and texts, is an issue yet to be reconciled to universal satisfaction. The question still remains, however, as to how to treat the obviously important issue of truth in the *Provinciales*. Common sense suggests that it be thematized and that it be considered as an internal device around which the *Lettres,* whether one deems them essentially fictional or not, are organized and out of which they were generated. Across the *Lettres* comes the unrelenting message that in their propogation of Molinism and the exaggerated form of casuistry deriving from it, the Jesuits are corruptors of truth and purveyors of truthlessness. In this light, Molinist disruptions of ordinary language, linguistic convention, and common sense do not represent abstract intellectual problems for Pascal; they are fundamental aggressions against truth itself. Edouard Morot-Sir makes the point that Pascal's obsessive quest for truth is not only indistinguishable from the rhetorical choices he himself makes, but that language itself is coextensive with that quest.[2]

In the *Provinciales* the issue of truth can be seen as operating on two intersecting axes: *adequatio* and *aletheia.* The first of these, which we have already seen to a more or less explicit degree in Pascal's analyses of his adversaries' positions, has to do with praxis, with the truthful use of language. Subtending his argument right from the beginning is the premise that words generally and theological terms specifically are supposed to line up with meanings and applications available commonly to those who use the terms. The words *grâce suffisante* are supposed to refer to a grace that suffices, not to a grace that has to be supplemented in order to suffice. The term "heretic" is supposed to designate someone who attacks doctrine, not someone who attacks the Jesuit order. To take an oath is to give one's word as bond. That is how the notion of oath, and hence the oath itself, is understood by the person receiving it. And he understands it that way because the concept conforming to the commonly held sense of the word itself leads him to do so. On this level, then, Pascal's service to truth lies in his dedication to the reestablishment of a correct functional rapport between word and referent, between what is said and what is meant. In short, he looks to valorize in the eyes of his readers and at the expense of his adversaries, the notion of adequacy: adequacy of the elements of language to themselves and adequacy of language to the basic tenets of Catholicism, to which that language applies and which it serves. Taken in a broader sense, adequation does not merely indicate tidiness of language and accuracy of usage. It indicates, indeed expresses, truth itself; for the concept of adequation is intimately associated with our own common understanding of the concept of truth itself. The classical definition is as follows: *veritas est adequatio intellectus et rei*. Truth is adequation or conformity of an intellectual representation and a referent. So, if, as in the case of the Molinists, this rapport of conformity has been violated, it is not simply a matter of violence to linguistic usage, it is already an attempt on truth itself. In the *Provinciales*, this truth we call adequation—Pascal himself does not use the term—will be associated with common sense, that is, to a logic naturally perceptible to sincere men.

The correlation of truth and common sense for Pascal is clarified in the following argument against one of the casuist rationalizations for homicide:

> Les permissions de tuer, que vous accordez en tant de rencontres, font paraître qu'en cette matière vous avez tellement oublié la loi de Dieu, et tellement éteint les lumières naturelles, que vous avez besoin qu'on vous remette dans les principes les plus simples de la religion et du sens commun; car qu'y a-t-il de plus naturel que ce sentiment *qu'un particulier n'a pas droit sur la vie d'un autre? Nous en sommes tellement instruite de nous-mêmes*, dit saint Chryostome, *que, quand Dieu a établi le précepte de ne point tuer, il n'a pas ajouté que c'est à cause que l'homicide est un mal; parce,* dit ce Père, *que la loi suppose qu'on a déjà appris cette vérité de la nature.* (Letter 14, p. 187)

When the casuist "accords" permission to kill, he is not simply authorizing or giving permission; he is, as the verb Pascal uses suggests, effecting a reconciliation of a base urge for vengeance or advantage with the law that had forbidden satisfaction of that very urge. And if this accord can be said to cut the heart out of the law—one of the principal semic components of *accorder* is *cor/cordis*: heart—it is precisely because this supposed permission insults two sources certifying that homicide cannot be justified. And one of those sources is common sense, that is, an immediately perceptible argument expressing a sense of the community that rebukes the premise that "un particulier [ait] le droit sur la vie d'un autre." The numerous authorizations of homicide put forth by the casuists are as much an affront to human law and to man's sense of dignity as to God's law. What is more, this sense of a prohibition held commonly as true and authentic is, in Pascal's text, given equal rhetorical footing with divine law. This is not to say that the two are in essence equivalent, but rather that they are in fundamental accord, the one being the extension of the other. In other words, there is nothing fundamentally mysterious about God's law. In this example, divine proscription against killing stands as an affirmation of a "pre-existing" natural truth, an intuition already in place, already assimilated by clear thinking men, and already incorporated into the social order to which they subscribe. Indeed, the divine law would be a fundamental, simple articulation of the truth of natural law. Pascal makes this same point in another place where, quoting Saint Augustine, he equates God's law and natural law: "[...] recherchez, mes frères, ce qui suffit à l'ouvrage de Dieu, c'est-à-dire à la nature..." (Letter 12, p. 166). In the case of homicide, there is no reason to explain, and certainly no need to justify, divine law. It would be overly simplistic and redundant to point out the evil of homicide, since an understanding of that evil is already incorporated into man's sense of the way things have to be ("nous en sommes tellement instruits de nous-mêmes").

From this same observation on homicide, the second axis along which the notion of truth in the *Provinciales* operates, can then be isolated. If, as is suggested in Pascal's analysis, authentic common sense derives from "nature," then to "extinguish" the natural light of reason would be analogous to "forgetting" the laws of God. ("Les permissions de tuer, que vous accordez [...] font paraître qu'en cette matière vous avez tellement *oublié la loi de Dieu, et tellement éteint les lumières naturelles* [...]" (emphasis mine). Common sense makes sense precisely because a principle, in this case, an interdiction against the taking of life, has already been established in the natural order of things, an order that anticipates God's law, just as God's law formalizes that same order. To forget God's law, which is what Pascal accuses the casuist of doing, is to go against nature, that is, against the truth of nature. Now, the other classical definition of truth is intimately connected with the notion of forgetting, specifically with the movement away from forgetfulness:

> "Vérité" a toujours voulu dire deux choses. [...] vérité est d'une part dévoilement de ce qui se tient caché dans l'oubli (*alétheia*), voile soulevé, relevé, de la chose même, de ce qui est comme trou déterminable de l'être; d'autre part (mais cet autre procès est préinscrit dans le premier [...] la vérité est accord (*homoisis* ou *adequatio*), rapport de ressemblance ou d'égalité entre une re-présentation et une chose (présent dévoilé), eventuellement dans l'énoncé d'un jugement.[3]

At the risk of oversimplifying matters, it will be possible to shuttle back and forth between the metaphysical concept of *aletheia*, or at least its suggestiveness, and its theological analogue, revealed truth. As Heinrich Fries notes: "*Re-velare* is quite specific in concept: it means to take away the *velum*, or veil, or cover. It means to make known, to reveal openly; what was previously covered and invisible in now 'lifted up' into sight."[4] One of the tasks to which Pascal consecrates himself in the *Provinciales* is to make sure that this truth remains painfully visible to those who would have forgotten it, who would have intentionally obscured it in the machinery of a new theology. This revealed truth is the *temoignage*, the testimony that proves or makes the case. It is the evidence, that is, what is seen clearly by those who look in the proper direction. In this sense, the writer of the letters makes frequent allusions and appeals to a truth that has the qualities of a preexisting, active, and comprehensible entity. It is this truth that can be qualified as revealed.[5] The demands and the accusations he makes in the name of common sense and of the proper use of language would be correlative to, and guaranteed by, this larger sense of truth. The operations of *adequatio* are, in Pascal's view, local manifestations of a truth already existing before and beyond them. So the reader of the *Provinciales* is enjoined to accept the reality of an hypostasized truth working as an operative principle of Pascal's argument. It is from this sense of truth that the operations of adequation take their cue, and it is towards this truth that the *Provinciales* claim to orient themselves. It will be important, then, to identify what the polemicist wants his readers, and especially his adversaries, to retrieve from their forgetfulness. What does he presuppose when, for example, he uses the term "truth" in his warnings to the Jesuits that they will not escape him, that they will feel the "force of the truth" he bears against them?

The first and most obvious quality of this larger and active truth is the irreducible distance between it and untruth or untruthful behavior. In this regard, the thought that truth could in some way be served by its antithesis is for Pascal an essential impossibility. He makes this point in Letter 11, where he sets out criteria for determining whether our animadversions ("nos repréhensions") originate in piety and charity or in impiety and hatred. The rule he reports comes from the Church Fathers who would represent wholly reliable transmitters of truth: "[...] l'esprit de piété porte toujours à parler avec vérité et sincérité; au lieu que l'envie et la haine

emploient le mensonge et la calomnie" (Letter 11, p. 154). He then goes
on to observe that

> quiconque se sert du mensonge agit par l'esprit du diable. Il n'y a point
> de direction d'intention qui puisse rectifier la calomnie: et quand il
> s'agirait de convertir toute la terre, il ne serait pas permis de noircir les
> personnes innocentes; parce qu'on ne doit pas faire le moindre mal pour
> en faire réussir le plus grand bien, et *que la vérité de Dieu n'a pas
> besoin de notre mensonge*, selon l'Ecriture. *Il est du devoir des
> défenseurs de la vérité*, dit Saint Hilaire, *de n'avancer que des choses
> vraies*. (Letter 11, p. 155)

In his exposition of the qualities of truth, Pascal holds to a
fundamental incompatibility between the truth and lies. So basic is this
incompatibility that the greatest good cannot justify the slightest evil. By
definition, the two categories exclude one another. This sort of exclusion
finds its analogue in Pascal's conservative linguistics and in the stringency
of his logic. Just as *suffisante* can never mean *insuffisante;* and just as
simony or assassination cannot signify anything that deprives them of the
sense by which all men define the terms, lies and slander cannot be brought
to the service of truth. In his discussion of Jesuit recourse to lies in the
business of repopulating the Church, Pascal's argument takes an interesting
turn. At one point he alludes to the essential incompatibility between God's
truth and the untruthful activity not only of the Jesuits, but of people
generally ("la vérité de Dieu n'a pas besoin de *notre* mensonge"). To
lie—or to be capable of lying—is as human as is to err. To remain exclusively "human"—and Pascal will constantly indict the fundamentally
"human" concerns of his adversaries' moral agenda— is to respond not
only to the demands of appetite or concupiscence, it is also to remain close
to the attraction of "our lies." Pascal's sense of truth as the necessary
course demands a rejection of the kind of discourse promoted by the
casuists, precisely because it is designed to serve human desire in an
exclusive way.[6]

By contrast, his own discourse would be the discourse of truth
insofar as it responds to the duty that Saint Hilairy ascribes to defenders of
truth; namely, that such defenders put forth only true propositions ("de
n'avancer que des choses vraies"). Pascal has clearly positioned himself in
the camp of defenders of truth. His sources, referees not only of his
argument in its large lines, but of this local argument on the subject of truth,

are to be considered as irreproachable as the Jesuits' self-referential and self-serving casuist models are to be considered suspect. For Pascal, there would be the same fundamental gap between the discourse of scripture or the writings of the Church Fathers and the aberrant casuist texts, as there is between truth and lies. This is not to say that the whole concept and the slightest detail of casuistry are based on untruth, that all casuists engage in lies or teach error. It is to say, rather, that Pascal perceives a substantial break between the absolute authority of texts sanctioned by Church tradition and the novelties of a system that extends beyond the bounds of reasonableness into the domain of rationalization. This break has to do with the reliability of the two sets of texts. The casuist texts, operating always in a relative, tightly defined way, do not link up directly with the source of truth. On the other hand, Scripture and the writings of the Church Fathers cannot be in error, precisely because they are part of an unfragmented sequence, an unbroken link with the source of truth, with the divine.

From this perspective, Pascal underscores what is basically a medieval conception of truth and its place in a theological sense of the world:

> The medieval conception of knowledge yokes the knowledge of beings under the doctrine of faith, which reserves for itself all final and genuine knowledge. To know about beings in this scheme of things is to know them in relation to a creator [...]. Since the primary reference of the medieval knowledge of beings derived from the revealed works of the church, which had as their central object of concern the knowledge of the supreme being, knowledge of beings became a reflection of the knowledge of the supreme being, and, consequently, a theology. The expression of this theological knowledge was found in documents that were believed to be direct revelations of God. Truth itself was understood as a revelation of God and knowledge of the truth of beings was achieved through an examination of the documents that contained the revealed truths.[7]

One of Pascal's underlying premises in the *Provinciales* is that the Jesuits, in their rejection of the presuppositions and implications of Augustinian thinking on grace, and in their promulgation of exaggerated forms of casuistry, have opened up a gap between their texts and the sacred texts in which truth is revealed as such. This gap is the distance and the difference between two sets of readings. On the human side of the gap, the texts and traditions of truth are obscured and forgotten under the weight of desire, self-love, and appetite. The gap separates man from the ways of God and gives privilege to his own logic, to a chronologic that responds in a relative way to the demands of particular times and places. In this regard, it is not without interest that part of the shock value Pascal gives to his exhibition of casuist moral pronouncements rests in the fact that these pronouncements shamelessly specify time and place, as, for example, in the maxims governing fasting, near occasions of sin, and one's obligation to love God.

In moving even further away from the general applicability of the original texts; by turning to their own authors as authority and precedent, the Jesuits give the human logic of casuistry ever increasing jurisdiction and privilege. And this self-reliance and self-reflexivity, which pushes the casuists to deal not only with an infinitely open series of cases, but which also ends up obliging them to reconcile contradictory positions of their own authors, will also move them further away from a second basic feature of truth, namely, its simplicity. The offense to simplicity is a natural and unavoidable consequence of the doctrine of probabilism that allows the Jesuits to justify in the same breath opinions at once conforming to, and at odds with, not only the sense of the Church's teaching, but also with the intuitive understanding of their own theologians:

> Concluons donc, mes Pères, que puisque votre probabilité rend les bons sentiments de quelques-uns de vos auteurs inutiles à l'Eglise, et utiles seulement à votre politique, ils ne servent qu'à nous montrer, par leur contrariété, la duplicité de votre cœur, que vous nous avez parfaitement découverte, en nous déclarant d'une part que Vasquez et Suarez sont contraires à l'homicide, et de l'autre, que plusieurs auteurs célèbres sont pour l'homicide, afin d'offrir deux chemins aux hommes, en détruisant la simplicité de l'Esprit de Dieu, qui maudit ceux qui sont doubles de cœur, et qui se préparent deux voies: *Voe duplici corde, et ingredienti duabus viis.* (Letter 13, p. 186)

The violence to truth is therefore not reconciled by the occasional orthodox opinion put forth by a "serious" casuist. Indeed, it is precisely because the correct path is sometimes indicated that probabilism is all the more pernicious. In this sense the doctrine bears a clear resemblance to the disorienting qualities Pascal will ascribe in the *Pensées* to imagination.[8]

The simplicity that Pascal valorizes as an essential constituant of truth, of this "esprit de Dieu," is an indication not only of its obviousness and the ease with which it is to be apprehended, but also of its indivisibility (*simplicitas*). The simplicity of God's proscriptions against homicide, for example, also prefigures the directness of the malediction against those who would destroy that simplicity. ("[...] L'Esprit de Dieu, qui maudit ceux qui sont doubles de cœur, et qui se préparent deux voies."[9]) Casuist probabilism has fragmented the single, simple "esprit de Dieu"—esprit being the spirit, the heart, the sense, the essence—into two roads that while contradictory, would supposedly be equally viable. In doing this, it has also nullified—at least for those who seek such nullification—the true way, insofar as that way is *defined* precisely as simple and indivisible. The right direction, the *bon sens*, is a single direction, and the other road, the one that splits and splits off from it, cannot be taken as an alternative or parallel road, it is fraudulent (*duplicitas*) and misleading. It is as fraudulent and misleading as the logic of numbers and quantity—logical ramifications of a principle such as probabilism whose fundamental operation lends itself to duplication and to the generation of multiple paths of morality.

The two ways, the one supported by Pascal, and the one proffered by the casuists, are dramaticaly juxtaposed in the course of an exchange between Montalte and the Jesuit over the issue of determining the value of a human life itself. In response to Montalte's "curiosity"—he wants to know why a precise sum has not yet been fixed—the Jesuit protests that such a determination, no mean chore, will give a palpable sense of the need for casuist wisdom, especially in the face of patristic adherence to and transmission of an uncomplicated proscription against killing. Pascal's quoting ("*non occides* ") and immediate translation of this direct language, situated as it is within the context of casuistic quantification, assures that the truth of the commandment stands in bold relief on Pascal's page, in his argument, and in the consciousness of his reader. The power of the scriptural language resides precisely in the unqualified expressing of what it has to say. This expressing reaches back through the language of the Church Fathers to the language passed down directly from God to man. It points, then, to another aspect of the truth underwriting and energizing Pascal's argument, namely its durability. Referring to the Jesuits' ploy of avowing or disavowing their own maxims solely in terms of the repercussions that unbending adherence to them might have on the prestige of the order, Pascal will enter into evidence the distinction between truth and the chronologic of his adversaries: "et ainsi vous les reconnaissez ou les renoncez, non pas selon la vérité qui ne change jamais, mais selon les divers changements des temps, suivant cette parole d'un ancien: *Omnia pro tempore, nihil pro veritate*" (Letter 12, p. 164). This notion of change is reiterated almost verbatim in Letter 15 where, once again, the Jesuits stand accused of waffling on their positions—an impossibility in Pascal's own approach—and agree that a certain maxim does or does not appear in their books, or that it is good or evil "non selon la vérité, qui ne change jamais, mais selon [leur] intérêt, qui change à toute heure" (Letter 15, p. 209). Since in both formulations truth ("qui ne change jamais") is a constant, the second term can, by dint of a simple algebra, be considered rhetorically interchangeable. To Pascal's way of thinking, the Jesuits' self-interest is much the same thing as the "divers changements des temps." In both cases the accent is put on instability. Intent and time, in this case, local, imminent time, are both highly relative concepts. They are accidental, degraded versions of the absolute, essential conceptions that Pascal promotes.

Attention to this simple, clear and enduring truth would be sufficient to re-establish unity and harmony in the Church, since the principles reflected in that truth would apply in a blanket way to the practices of the faith. Pascal underscores the point in Letter 13 when he challenges his adversaries with this question:

> N'est-il pas vrai, mes Pères, que si vous regardiez véritablement Dieu, et que l'observation de sa foi fût le premier et principal objet de votre pensée, ce respect regnerait uniformément dans toute vos décisions importantes, et vous engagerait à prendre dans toutes ces occasions l'intérêt de la religion? (p. 182)

To be observant of truth, to be attentive to the demands of faith is to "regarder véritablement Dieu." Pascal's recourse to the semantics of vision—something he does frequently in the *Provinciales* and elsewhere in his work—underscores the implicit notion that the truth he holds up as the model from which moral and theological systems are to be generated is, in fact, an evidential truth. It reveals itself directly to the soul's faculties of perception. And if, as Pascal exhorts his Jesuits to do, this truth is kept in view—"observed" (in both senses of the term)—if God is "regardé véritablement," the respect born of this attentiveness will naturally and uniformly apply in practice and will target the single interest of religion, not the multiple interests of the Society of Jesus.

Obviously, Pascal's preoccupation with truth is not with an abstraction floating serenely above the heat and the anger of the polemic in which he is engaged. Nor, for all his outrage at the aberrant prescriptions and counsels of his adversaries, does he propose simply that the casuists be excluded. Of course, he does condemn the excesses of what he deems to be a system at odds with the best interest and the traditions of the Church; and he has no qualms about positing a diabolical origin for that system. At the same time, however, he does point out his own good and constructive intentions. He qualifies his own attacks on, and denuding of, the casuist writings as part of a program of unification; which is to say, as a reflection of one of the principal qualities of the truth to which he subscribes and to which his argument appeals.

> Je voudrais bien, mes Pères, que ce que je vous dis servît non seulement à me justifier, ce serait peu, mais encore à vous faire sentir et abhorrer ce qu'il y a de corrompu dans les maxims de vos casuistes, afin de nous unir sincèrement dans les saintes règles de l'Evangile, selon lesquelles nous devons être tous jugés. (Letter 12, p. 166)

Pascal sees fit, then, to make an important distinction between the local interest of his own text and a larger, more significant issue of the Jesuits' relationship to the texts they have adopted. In this distinction is a clear evocation of the two categories of truth, *adequatio* and *aletheia*, at stake in the *Provinciales*.

When Pascal maintains his wish that what he has to say be useful in justifying his own writing, he refers not only to the adequacy of his research, that is, to his own harvesting and manipulating of quotations, or to his exploitation of the material at his disposal; but also to the general stance he takes. As he points out, in an almost whimsical way, this would be a matter of small concern ("ce serait peu"); for, in effect, he is wholly convinced of the rectitude of his stand and the presuppositions upon which it is based. On the other hand, a more meaningful, indeed, a momentous accomplishment, would be that his work move the Jesuits to *sentir* and then to *abhorrer* the corrupt features of the maxims adopted in the casuist texts. These verbs are both richer than they might appear at first glance. The Jesuits would, if Pascal's desire be satisfied, first come to *feel* the impropriety of the counsel they give. This feeling is not exactly the same thing as intellectual or logical acceptance. Indeed, the Jesuit responses to the *Provinciales* have already demonstrated to Pascal that the logic of his own rationalistic and orderly approach has failed to move his adversaries to such acceptance. But the things that reason sometimes refuses to accept is sometimes able to touch the reasoning of the heart; and, in a sense, it is to the heart that Pascal appeals here. His hope is for something like an instinctive apprehension of a casuistry gone out of control. As Paul Bénichou notes, the real source of certainty is not reason, but rather something completely different: "cœur, instinct, lumière naturelle, tels sont les noms que Pascal donne à cette faculté intuitive, seule capable selon lui, d'affirmer, de poser quelque chose [...].[10] This apprehension, being felt and not just simply understood, would be a matter of the heart, as would the second component of the wish Pascal sets down here: that the Jesuits come to abhor the maxims.

The abhorrence that Pascal wants to provoke in the Jesuits is very much in tune with the notion of sensation expressed in *sentir:* to abhor is, of course, to detest, but it is also to feel in a physical way—in this case, the horror of the corruption inherent in the casuist texts. To abhor is to feel one's hair stand on end—abhor is linked etymologically to horror, itself linked to the notions of bristling and shuddering (*hérisser* in French); it is a physiological reaction to the most shocking kind of stimuli. The laying open of the corruptions of casuistry—corruptions deemed horrible precisely because they fragment (*co/rompre*: to break) the standing, integral laws and traditions of the Church as well as the prerogatives of common sense—is to move the Jesuits to distance themselves from the source of their horror. And, in point of fact, that is what Pascal's verb is able to convey. In its primitive sense the term "abhor," from *abhorrere*, already connotes a shrinking away from. Moreover, this movement away from that which disgusts, in this case, from the corrupt and corrupting prescriptions on morality, is, if we continue to exploit the original sense of the term "abhor," linked also to the notions of inconsistency and inappropriateness.[11] The Jesuits would, it is suggested, back away from ("abhor") these devisive orders of casuistry precisely because they would have come to an instinctive sense (*sentir*) of the inappropriateness, the *non-adequatio* of their logic to the basic codes of moral propriety.

The recoil that Pascal hopes will issue from his writing would take his adversaries back across the gap separating their moral principles (and the theological presuppositions underpinning them) from the laws and truth bearing the mark of the divine and transmitted through the authoritative channels, specified repeatedly as Scripture, the popes, and the councils.

Indeed, the goal Pascal sets before his adversaries is the possibility of nothing less than a complete shrinking of the gap, of a complete reconstruction of that which had been fragmented. He is, in fact, looking to a unification of the two adversarial camps. If the Jesuits can be moved to abhor the corruption of their method, they will come to be united "sincerely" with Pascal and the Jansenists, whom he qualifies as adhering to the "saintes règles de l'Evangile, selon lesquelles nous devons tous être jugés." Implicit in this reference to the final judgment is a sense of the unmoving nature of the rules laid down in scripture. Implicit, also, is the thought, which is also a reminder, that those laws apply equally to those who accept them and to those who willfully, but inconsequentially, choose to disregard them.

Pascal sees his own text then as offering to the perverters of the unicity of the Catholic religion the possibility of seeing the light, of coming to their common senses and of turning away from the *mauvaise piste*. In other words, he qualifies his polemical activity as therapeutic, as a bitter pill that the purveyors of error and untruth will have to swallow if they are to reap its salvific benefits. The turning away from the extravagance and error of casuistry is a turn towards truth. It is, in short, a conversion. And if Pascal uses this term only rarely in the *Provinciales*, there is little doubt that he does insist on this medicinal, conversional feature of his undertaking. He is most emphatic on this in Letter 11, where in defense of his own editorial and rhetorical strategies, he presents to his Jesuit respondants an etiquette for proper recourse to sharp criticism. Among the rules he sets down is one that calls for discretion in the development of the case against one's adversary. It is not enough, Pascal opines, simply to tell the truth. One must at the same time demur from saying all the truths one has at one's disposal. Indeed, as Pascal sees it, this proviso would enjoy the same qualitative status as telling the truth ("mais ce n'est pas assez de ne dire que des choses vraies, il faut encore ne pas dire toutes celles qui sont vraies"). The reasoning behind this call for discretion is linked to the notion of usefulness, which itself takes as point of departure a sense of charity that would not want to "blesser sans apporter aucun fruit." The Jesuit texts that Pascal calls upon are, of course, chosen to cause discomfort to their proponents. They are designed to wound, but in a way that would bring the fruit of conversion.

A few paragraphs later Pascal unveils the fundamental presupposition of the rules he applies to his own project: "Pour abréger ces règles, je ne vous dira plus que celle-ci; qui est le principe et la fin de toutes les autres: c'est que l'esprit de charité porte à avoir dans le cœur le désir du salut de ceux contre qui on parle" (Letter 11, p. 156). In a sense Pascal provides here his own "direction of intention"; something that is perhaps even clearer in the quote from Augustine upon which he bases his contention. Augustine maintains that

> on doit toujours conserver la charité dans le cœur, lors même qu'on est obligé de faire au-dehors des choses qui paraissent rudes aux hommes, et de les frapper avec une aprêté dure, mais bien faisante, leur utilité devant être préférée à leur satisfaction. (p. 156)

Now, Pascal's attack may continue to be furious, relentless, and sharp; but to hear him tell it, his heart is in the right place and on the right track. Simultaneous to the aggressive discourse with which he attacks and seeks to destabilize his adversaries is another discourse, a prayer, directed to God. By underscoring the simultaneity of these two discourses,[12] Pascal is able to characterize his own project as something like a long and ongoing prayer. The text he submits to the Jesuits—and to which he submits them—is the external manifestation (in the quote from Augustine, it had been a question of being obliged to do what on the surface—"au-dehors"—appears rude) of an internal and heartfelt motif of charity, which is to say, the love of one's *prochain*. In this sense, the attack amounts to an empirical corollary to the thought that had closed the first letter. There Pascal washed his hands of the subversive and oppressive terms *pouvoir prochain,* saying that he could not persecute his *prochain* under such a pretext.

    Pascal's protestation of a charitable impulse is not made in the abstract; and he is quick to situate his own writing in this perspective of charity, maintaining as he does that there is nothing in his letters to suggest (*témoigner*) that he does not desire the salvation of the Jesuits or that he does not in effect pray to God for them. And since there is no evidence to the contrary, the Jesuits are obliged by the same demands of charity, which entails both a love of God and a love of one's *prochain,* to respect the premise that the composer of the letters does in fact have their real interest at heart. What Pascal does here is, in a sense, to sanctify his project by establishing an intimate and functional relationship between his charity and his attack. Charity is not only the motor behind his attacks, it is also the category, the authority, and the organizing principle by which Pascal would force his opponents to accept his text and its positions. In other words, charity, like truth, is a non-negotiable constant. It is a categorical imperative to which Pascal appeals, as much for tactical as for theological reasons. What he is in fact doing is appropriating the notion of charity, and applying it in such a way to the particular case of his own writing, that the Jesuits, provided they are playing fair, would be required to give him the benefit of the doubt: his writing would pain them, but the pain would be part of the therapy. Given the terms Pascal has established to his advantage and their application to his writing, the Jesuits should be hard pressed, on a public relations as well as on a theological level, to debunk the notion of charity.

By assuming control over the real definition of the term, Pascal has been able to place a formidable obstacle before his opponents. They cannot, in principle, deny the appropriateness of the category he establishes as part of the ground rules; and if they cannot displace the category, then they will have to swallow the bitter pill of his good intentions. Moreover, they will not be able to attack his writing by accusing it of hatred and partisan bias, primarily because the evidence points in to the contrary. As this evidence, or at least Pascal's claim to it, points to his own lack of uncharitable intent and practice, it also points out the Jesuits' own rhetorical opposition to the charity that wants to work for the salvation of one's adversary. The Jesuits will stand accused of violating, or as Pascal puts it, of "sinning," not only against the rules prescribing truthfulness, discretion, and propriety, but also against the general, all-encompassing, rule of charity.

In contrast to his own writing, where at no time can it be shown that he does not have the ultimate interest of his adversaries at heart, the Jesuits have made a point of expressing textually and publicly their desire for the eternal damnation of the Jansenists.[13] In so doing, they have in fact advertised their subscription to the politics and "theology" of hatred, insofar as they violate the sense of charity, that is, the unselfishness that turns toward the good of others. From such a perspective, the lack of charity would be consistent with, and consequential to, the moral positions of the unfettered casuistry Pascal opposes, positions that valorize willfulness and personal glory as being not only for the taking, but, in a sense, as being part of a heroic model. And just as the maxims point to the primacy of an "ego oblige" simmering at the heart of the Jesuit brand of casuistry, the Jesuits' rhetoric of damnation unveils the heart of their politics. The Jesuit frankness on the subject has, in effect, given Pascal access to the innermost reaches of their politics. This frankness on the part of the Jesuit theoreticians stands in implicit but clear contrast to Pascal's own claims of discretion and charity. Moreover, in calling for the damnation of their opponents, the Jesuits have marked their own discourse, and, one can infer, their fundamental positions, as excessive, indiscrete, and uncharitable. What Pascal has been able to do here is to provide a corollary to his other principal act of sabotage against the casuist system—namely, his demonstration that the system allows and promotes lying. By implicating the casuists in cruelty, self-interest, and uncharitableness, he holds them up as worthy of neither credibility nor veneration.

The language of the Jesuits that would wish their adversaries straight to hell, is for Pascal the language of violence, which in the etiquette he establishes is as much the language of untruth as it is of uncharitableness and indecency. Violence is an incompatible substitute for truth. At the end of Letter 12, Pascal analyzes the confrontation of truth and violence, which would, of course, be the confrontation between his position and discourses against those of the Molinists. One of his main points is that there is nothing new to this confrontation: in its larger lines, it is already long-standing and it will doubtless continue.

> Vous croyez avoir la force et l'impunité mais je crois avoir la vérité et l'innocence. C'est une étrange et longue guerre que celle où la violence essaie d'opprimer la vérité. Tous les efforts de la violence ne peuvent affaiblir la vérité, et ne servent qu'à le relever davantage. Toutes les lumières de la vérité ne peuvent rien pour arrêter la violence, et ne font que l'irriter plus. Quand la force combat la force, la plus puissante détruit la moindre: quand l'on oppose les discours aux discours, ceux qui sont véritables et convaincants confondent et dissipent ceux qui n'ont que la vanité et le mensonge: mais la violence et la vérité ne peuvent rien l'une sur l'autre. Qu'on ne prétende pas de là néanmoins que les choses soient égales: car il y a cette extrême différence, que la violence n'a qu'un cours borné par l'ordre de Dieu, qui en conclut les effets à la gloire de la vérité qu'elle attaque: au lieu que la vérité subsiste éternellement, et triomphe enfin de ses ennemis, parce qu'elle est éternelle et puissante comme Dieu même. (Letter 12, p. 173)

This passage says much about the larger view in which the Jansenist/Jesuit struggle is imbedded, and of which it is but a local manifestation. Indeed, Pascal all but situates the struggle on the level of allegory. The obvious care he takes here justifies a detailed appreciation of his terms and their deployment. The immediate contextual springboard into the remarkable analysis of the struggle is a provisional refusal on the part of Pascal to take up the matter of false and scandalous attacks with which the Jesuits end their responses. Reserving that task for a later letter, he does make a point of pitying his adversaries for feeling obliged to take the low road ("je vous plains mes Pères, d'avoir recours à de tels remèdes") and of assuring his detractors that their personal attacks will do nothing to clarify differences, nor will threats stop him from defending his positions. It is here that the passage we examine in detail begins.

"Vous croyez avoir la force et l'impunité mais je crois avoir la vérité et l'innocence." At first glance the two parts of Pascal's complex sentence point in their formal symmetry to a basic equivalence between the two camps and the weapons they deploy. However, upon closer inspection, this sense of symmetry breaks down. The "mais" with which Pascal begins the second component of his discussion of "armaments" already destabilizes the symmetry. "But" is not the same as "and": the Jesuits may have force and impunity; Pascal has something else altogether. The rhetorical shift triggered by "mais" suggests, and also effects, a difference between the two uses of the verb "croire." The Jesuit "belief" in their possession of force and impunity is the kind of belief that in Pascal's view would, in fact, say "you may think you have possession over force and impunity, but I possess something else again, something that goes well beyond that: truth and innocence." This second aspect then rebounds back onto the first proposition, that is, on the Jesuits' position, weakening it precisely by inferring the lack of real symmetry or parity between the two combatants and their arms. This lack of parity is further enhanced in the semantic differentiation between innocence on one hand and impunity on the other. Significantly, these two terms will disappear from the text of the analysis after fulfilling this first differential function. Whereas truth and force may not *necessarily* be in an antagonistic relationship the one with the other, innocence and impunity seem to be already situated in a same semantic field where the common element is something like the legitimacy of one's action. The difference is, of course, that impunity represents the lower limit of such legitimacy. It entails just getting by, just slipping through the obstacles that would have imposed sanctions on the act in question, in this case an act of violence. Impunity does not really legitimize or underwrite force; it simply allows it to continue; it gives it an impulse and an energy that are merely formal. In short, impunity would, in the speciousness of the position Pascal ascribes to the Jesuits, be a warrant of force. This sense of getting by, of fulfilling the minimum requisites for pursuit of a course of action is not substantially different from the overall personality of the casuistry that Pascal takes to task, insofar as that system offers the minimum course for moral propriety.

On the other hand, innocence is a much broader concept. Unlike impunity, which operates as something of a technical demarcation, innocence defines a state that precedes and legitimizes the action and serves to define truth. To work within truth is to do its work and to be armed by it. The imbalance is already in place, already inscribed in the terms and, through them, in the positions of the adversaries. Despite the underlying inequality of the arms, the two combatants, truth and force, are said to be engaged in a long and strange war. The war extends beyond the participants of the present struggle, precisely because the present struggle is but an articulation of the assaults on truth come from a diversity of angles; the war is one in which truth has historically had to reassert and reconfirm its rightful place. The war is said also to be strange. The term is important, for it points not only to the singular nature of the ongoing struggle, but more fundamentally, to its extraneousness (*étrange* derives from the Latin *extraneus*). Despite its chronic nature, the struggle between force and truth is, nonetheless, outside the fundamental order of things. It does not come from any internal inconsistencies—truth stands solid, integral, and unchanging—but from forces bearing down from the outside. In this war, truth is attacked by something extraneous and alien to it; and the attempts that force makes on the edifice of truth are as ill-conceived as the fundamental gap between impunity and innocence.

What is most strange in the long, strange, and extraneous war is precisely that force takes pains to try and oppress truth; and the violence of force is specified as oppression, as an effort to push truth down, to put it under pressure and to prevent it from taking its rightful place as guarantor of correct action. Force would try to contain truth by covering it over—an image that suggests the contrary of the unveiling, openness, and liberation constitutive of truth as *aletheia*. But these *efforts*—and the term itself picks up the phonological, if not the semantic, resonance of the word "force," and may thus further punctuate the self-serving, self-referential objectives of force—are incapable of weakening truth, precisely because truth is itself a force, one that is resistant to the strain that the strange and extraneous war brings forcefully to bear upon it. Moreover, the efforts of that force serve only to lift truth higher, to underscore it, and to energize it ("la relever davantage"). Violence and truth are in an inverse functional relationship. Violence, being impertinent and inadequate, can only put truth into a clearer and more forceful position.

Going in the other direction, the inverse functional relationship gives similar, but not at all equivalent, results. Pascal writes: "toutes les lumières de la vérité ne peuvent rien pour arrêter la violence, et ne font que l'irriter plus." The effort of truth would thus be its *lumière,* its power to illuminate and clarify; but against violence this light is ineffective, since violence is, as the common expression has it, already blind. And as it flails around in the dark, in that wild place of un-enlightenment and refusal to come out of the darkness, the heat and the light of truth only makes violence all the more violent. Pascal uses the term *irriter.* Truth ends up irritating violence, pushing it further into the reaches and grasp of unthinking, unreasoning fury.

Pascal then presents the terms of more orthodox, less *étrange* contests: force against force; discourse against discourse. In the case of force, the stronger will naturally prevail; it will destroy the weaker. The matter of factness of this observation is underscored by the pared down simplicity of Pascal's expression. There is no need for elaboration. This elemental quality will be further highlighted when the question of discourse is taken up. Although the second idea initially parallels the first in terms of style ("quand l'on oppose les discours aux discours..."), it takes on details that render it richer, more precise and more damaging. If, in the analysis of forces pitted against each other, the characteristic of the "victorious" force was its superiority in the very thing that defines force—the most forceful (*puissante*) force will prevail—so too will the victorious discourse demonstrate and exploit its constitutive features, namely, veracity and persuasiveness. Truthfulness is an essential attribute of genuinely powerful discourse. From this perspective, it is not without some interest to his argument that, in identifying the victorious discourse, Pascal uses the verb "être," and thus establishes an ontological link between forceful discourse and truthful discourse. On the other hand, he uses the verb *avoir* to qualify the vanquished discourse, which would "have" but "vanité et mensonge." While authentic, adequate discourse is defined by truth and is equivalent to it, unauthentic discourse such as the one the Jesuits maintain and promulgate, would be discourse falsified by accidental attributes forced upon it by its corruptors and manipulators. These corruptors would not have access to the force inherent in correct discourse, a force that will always vanquish false discourse. Its power to vanquish (*vaincre*) is its power to convince (*convaincre*), a power that, in Pascal's view, will always manifest itself, as it does manifest itself in the opposition of his own discourse, which is the true discourse of scripture and Church tradition, to the self-satisfied and futile discourse of the casuists. The futility characteristic of this untruthful discourse is very much the same as futility of the strange war between force and truth.

This strangeness is linked also to the apparent stalemate between the two combatants: "la violence et la vérité ne peuvent rien l'une sur l'autre." In logical or earthbound terms, the incapacity of one of the ill-suited combatants to bring the war to resolution would indicate the validity of each side. This is, of course, a consideration based on relative categories. Pascal sees things in a larger, more absolute, way that stands firm against such hasty claims of parity between truth and violence. When Pascal warns his readers—and his Jesuits—not to "pretendre de là néanmoins que les choses soient égales," he is putting his reader on guard not only against making such claims, but also against pretentious, self-satisfied vanity. This sort of vanity leads to the kind of reductive thinking that would deflate the scope and significance of the struggle precisely by establishing parity between truth and violence.

In Pascal's view, the two combatants, force and truth, are not at all in a relationship of parity. Indeed, the difference between them is qualified as "extrême." It is essential to the thrust of Pascal's overall argument to understand this word as much more than a synonym of a term such as "très" or "important." What the polemicist means to get across is the irreconcilability of the values promulgated by force, violence, vanity, and lies, on the one hand, and those resumed in the notion of truth, on the other. The gap between the two adversaries, the Jansenists and the Molinists, and between the two combatants, truth and force, does not fall within the contracted margins of simple linguistic or ethical dispute. The gap is as wide as the *inadequatio*, the falsity of that strange struggle between truth and violence, between discourse that is truthful and discourse that relies on fraudulent linguistics, on the logic of quantity or on the excessive rationalizations of casuistry. Indeed, it is when discourse, brought into line with the original *logos* (the Word which is the name of wisdom, of the divine, of ratio and adequation) meets infinity, the number that extends beyond countability, that truth will triumph:

Il y a cette extrême différence que la violence n'a qu'un cours borné par
l'ordre de Dieu, qui en conduit les effets à la gloire de la vérité qu'elle
attaque, au lieu que la vérité subsiste éternellement et triomphe enfin de
ses ennemis, parce qu'elle est éternelle et puissante comme Dieu même.

At this juncture, truth will vanquish precisely because it is eternal and
powerful as God himself. This power enables it to *subsister,* to claim the
stability that is proper to it and to survive. "Subsister" means to remain
after the demise of something else, in this case, the violence of erroneous
discourse. The connotation here is of a durability beyond limited human
endeavor and of an inherent capacity to succeed—in both senses of the
term.

On the other hand, "tous les effets de la violence" are destined to
fail, precisely because they are limited by the constraints of the finite, by a
cours borné, a designation that in the argument of the *Provinciales* would
apply manifestly to the theology and moral codes of the Molinists. The
cours, a term that can signify at once the extension, the jurisdiction, and the
inherent worth of these efforts of violence, would be limited not only in its
applicability—casuistry would in the end be limited by its own self-
contradicting features[14]—but in its presuppositions. The radical casuistry
subtending and responding to Molinist theology is predicated on a basic
valorization of the human will. In this view, man would put his will and
reason to the service of his own good, and to a certain extent, Pascal would
agree. However, in agreeing, he would insist that the "good" sought in the
confusion of casuist maxims and prescriptions is itself limited. Like the
efforts of violence, the pursuit of local, temporal, and terrestrial good (e.g.,
preoccupation with wealth, the cult of honor, the sating of appetites) is *un
bien borné*, precisely because man himself would have chosen a course that
is limited. He would have taken on the device of his own imprisonment.
He would have opted for the course of least effort, which, in the argument Pascal proffers, would be the course of violence, of tendentious
rationalization, of slander, false accusation, defective language, and facile
quantification. These approaches to morality, linked intimately to faith in
the efficacy of the human will, end up causing man to turn in place, precisely because they seem to offer him a viable alternative to the call and the
demands of the infinite, of what he instinctively knows to be the truth, but
which he chooses to forget and cover over. What the Molinist approaches
do offer is the seductive thought that human reason is the true conduit to the

moral life. For Pascal, however, reason would be wholly impotent in the matter of morality.[15]

Across the *Provinciales* Pascal advocates the notion that Molinism and the excesses of casuistry attending it are at bottom willful and dangerous collaborations with the world, with "le language de la ville de trouble" (Letter 14, p. 198). Making such a choice, the proponents and disciples of Molinistic casuistry would, in Pascal's eyes, be doomed to remain stuck in the redundant, self-contradictory structures and demands of the world. At the same time, Pascal's text points to the possibility of conversion, that is, of a return to sources and to the truth contained in those sources. Indeed, one can say that the letters themselves underscore this notion of conversion in their very structure, a structure determined in large measure by the very refusal of the Jesuits to cede to Pascal's arguing. The responses to the early and middle letters force Pascal to rehash points already made. They force him to return once again to his own casuist sources to dredge up more textual support for his original allegations. This return to the points of departure would mesh with the very notion of conversion, which, in its original sense, denotes a turning around or a turning back. In the *Provinciales*, conversion, in addition to its theological resonance, would have the status of a trope; for *conversio* also signifies the rounding off of a period, the repetition at the end of a syntactic unit of the same word that had appeared at the beginning. And this is what happens in the *Provinciales*. Not only is there repetition of specific aspects of casuist moral codes, there is also a return in the final letters to the original point of departure, namely, the distinction between the *question de fait* and the *question de droit*, the matters of heresy and *pouvoir prochain*.

It could, of course, be argued that this return is born simply of frustration, that it points to the demise of the polemical enterprise taken up a year earlier. This argument would not be without a certain merit. All the same, it would be a mistake to read the recapitulation in the last letters as anything like a capitulation. It is, rather, an appeal—"laissez l'Eglise en paix"; a promise—"et je vous y laisserai de bon cœur"; and a warning— "mais pendant que vous ne travaillerez qu'à y entretenir le trouble, ne doutez pas qu'il ne se trouve des enfants de la paix qui se croiront obligés d'employer tous leurs efforts pour y conserver la tranquilité" (Letter 18. p. 269). And these "efforts," underscoring once again the futility of the Jesuits own "efforts de la violence," will be none other than the "force de la vérité" that Pascal promised in Letter 12. These efforts, and this is perhaps the strongest threat to the tranquility of the Jesuits themselves, may well be something very much like these same *petites lettres*, these *Lettres écrites à un ami provincial* that relentlessly and repeatedly strive for the violence of conversion by never compromising the principles of truth that subtend them and towards which they claim always to tend.

Notes

Chapter One

1. In his study, *Jansenism in Seventeenth Century France: Voices in the Wilderness* (Charlottesville: University of Virginia Press, 1977), Alexander Sedgwick makes the following point: "The significance of the *Provincial Letters* to the history of Jansenism is that they reasserted arguments pertaining to efficacious grace and contrition that had aroused the authorities of Church and state since the days of Saint-Cyran at the very moment when Mazarin and the papacy were trying to suppress those ideas" (p. 82).

2. René Rapin, *Mémoires [...] sur l'Eglise et la société, la cour, la ville et le jansénisme, 1644 1699* (Paris: Gaume Frères, 1865), II, p. 353.

3. The adherence of the theologian Baius to fundamental Augustinian principles was condemned by papal bull in 1567.

4. If Jansenism itself was doomed to violent attack (the Abbey at Port-Royal would be leveled by order of the King) and to the scandal of convulsionism, the system of casuistry that Pascal exposed so brilliantly and viciously would in the end be condemned and the Jesuit order expulsed from France.

5. Gérard Ferreyrolles: *Blaise Pascal: Les Provinciales* (Paris: Presses Universitaires de France, 1984), p. 8.

6. Jules Chaix-Ruy, *Le Jansénisme: Pascal et Port-Royal* (Paris: Librairie Felix Alcan, 1930), pp. 33-34.

7. Blaise Pascal, *Les Provinciales* (Paris: Garnier Frères, 1965), p. xxiv.

8. Blaise Pascal, *Lettres écrites à un provincial* (Paris: Garnier-Flammarion, 1981), p. 35. References to the *Provinciales* will be to this edition.

9. While there is no doubting that these passages are ripe with phonological data and that Pascal's prose very often resonates with a kind of poetic energy, some readers may balk at the assigning of meaning to this data. In defense of this manifestly literary approach—if a defense be necessary—I submit a bit of evidence which although circumstantial, is nonetheless germane. It was Pascal who proposed for the pedagogical program of Port-Royal's *petites écoles* a method for teaching reading that was based on the sound of the letters rather than on their names. Such professional interest in applied phonology could not help but spill over, if indirectly, into his own writing, especially in

a text such as the *Provinciales* where, in a manner of speaking, Pascal is demonstrating a way of reading the language of his adversaries.

10. In Letter 3, Pascal will underscore the frenzied aspect of the assault on Arnauld when he dramatizes the deployment of forces as "tant de docteurs acharnés sur un seul" (p. 56).

11. In Letter 2, Pascal will exploit the "logic" of the greatest number when in underscoring the ideological inconsistency of the Dominican alliance with the proponents of sufficient grace, he states that the alliance, because it makes for the greatest number, cannot help but give the impression that the Dominicans are *substantively* in agreement with a doctrine they have traditionally rejected. "Ils [the Dominicans] s'unissent à eux; ils font par cette union le plus grand nombre; ils se séparent de ceux qui nient les grâces suffisantes; ils déclarent que tous les hommes en ont. Que peut-on penser de là, sinon qu'ils autorisent les Jésuites" (Letter 2, p. 48).

12. Saint-Gilles, *Journal*, ed. Ernest Jovy (Paris: J. Vrin, 1936), p. 80.

13. "Rappelez dans votre mémoire les cabales, les factions, les erreurs, les schismes, les attentats qu'on leur reproche depuis si longtemps; de quelle sorte on les a décriés et noircis dans les chairs et dans les livres, et combien ce torrent, qui a eu tant de violence et de durée, était grossi dans ces dernières années, où on les accusait ouvertement et publiquement d'être non seulement hérétiques et schismatiques, mais apostats et infidèles, de nier de la transubstantion, et de renoncer à Jésus-Christ et à l'Evangile" (Letter 3, pp. 54-55). The reader cannot help but remark that virtually every substantive element of this declaration is, at the very minimum, doubled or tripled. Pascal seems to want to highlight stylistically the logic of quantification used by Port-Royal's adversaries as a supplement to the feableness and falsity of their complaint.

14. One of the seminal texts of the ongoing conflict between Jansenists and Molinists is Arnauld's *De la fréquente communion* (1643). In this work, Arnauld reiterates the argument put forth earlier by Saint-Cyran that receiving communion should be a rare occurence, and that preparation for it be long and severe. Among these preparations would be infrequent recourse to the sacrament of penance.

15. Letter 10, p. 139. The quote is in fact a quote—from the order's own history of its first century—and not lines fed to a fictional Jesuit voice.

16. The proviso that a respectful public countenance be maintained adds an element of theatricality to the maxim and allows us to see in it, if only in an associative way, a reflection of Jesuit pedagogical thinking. Leisure and diversion, considered essential to a sound education, first took the form of small theatrical productions by students for the amusement and edification of their classmates. Before long, however, the productions were opened up to an increasingly wider public, became more lavish, and abandonned Latin for the local tongue.

17. This phenomenon, part of the general tactic of displacement known as the direction of intention, will be studied more closely in a section dealing specifically with casuistic violence to linguistic convention and tradition.

18. In his wide-ranging study of the Church in the seventeenth century, Daniel-Rops delimits one of the dominant tendencies of the period: the growing separation between religion and daily existence. This fragmentational tendency had a clear and definite effect on moral principles. "Même chez les meilleurs une certaine intériorisation [the direction of intention would be a codified instance of this], à laquelle a contribué le courant spirituel du début du siècle, aboutit à cette sorte de scisson intime; une foi très vive peut aller de pair avec des attitudes en substance peu chrétiennnes [...]. Cette scisson entre la foi et la vie, la littérature l'a trahie—et l'art aussi nous le verrons. Pour être un héros cornélien faut-il être un chrétien? Sauf dans Polyeucte, où sont encore les vertus évangéliques de ces personnages si forts sur le point d'honneur, *si portés à la vengeance?* " (emphasis added). Daniel-Rops: *L'Eglise des temps classiques* (Paris: Fayard, 1958), p. 292.

19. "Vous avez ouï le langage de la ville de paix, qui s'appelle *la Jérusalem mystique*, et vous avez ouï le langage de la ville de trouble, que l'Ecriture appelle *la Spirituelle Sodome*: lequel de ces deux langages entendez-vous?" (Letter 14, p. 198).

Chapter Two

1. The question of an unfailing efficacious grace is, of course, as fundamental to the psychology of Jansenism as it is to its theology. Indeed, efficacious grace is wholly consonant with an austerity and pessimism founded in an unflinchingly realistic view of man. Paul Bénichou puts it this way: "La doctrine de la grâce efficace repose sur une représentation particulièrement sombre du péché originel et de la chute qui l'a suivi. Mais une idée aussi entière de la chute n'est, en fait, que la mise en œuvre théologique d'un parti pris de défiance et de sévérité envers l'homme tel qu'il est sous nos yeux, envers sa nature et ses impulsions. La doctrine de la grâce efficace est liée à une certaine attitude accusatrice de l'humanité, et elle en est l'achèvement spéculatif et métaphysique plutôt que la source" (*Morales du grand siècle*, pp. 125-26).

2. "Je crois qu'il [the term *pouvoir prochain*] n'a été inventé que pour brouiller" (Letter 1, p. 38).

3. Philip Lewis, "Dialogic Impasse in Pascal's *Provinciales*," *Canadian Review of Comparative Literature*, Winter (1976): p. 36.

4. "La Société est bien satisfaite de leur complaisance" (Letter 2, p. 45).

5. Specialists are divided over the identity of the respondant. They are, however, less unsure about the source of the two quotes that appear in this curious text. The first is thought to be either Chapelain or Gomberville (see Louis Cognet, ed., *Les Provinciales* [Paris: Garnier Frères, 1965], pp. 36-37) while the second, according to Racine and others, is probably Mme de Scudéry. To associate "real" names with the praise for the letters does not necessarily mean that the context in which they are placed shares the same status of nonfiction.

6. It is on this point that the identity of the respondant is significant; for the response is dated February 2, 1656, two days *after* the ouster of Arnauld from the Sorbonne. To refer to the censure as if it is yet to happen gives Pascal a certain rhetorical edge, insofar as he can reiterate apparently *before the fact* that the censure is of much less consequence than some might want—or need—to think.

7. In the text of the Letter, Pascal italicizes the term, thus providing a visual attenuation of the charge of heresy by shunting it off into the realm of conjecture.

8. By way of example, Pascal notes that at first the supposed heresy was based on the content of the five propositions; next it concerned the specific language of Jansenius's formulations ("le mot à mot"); afterwards it was a matter of the sense of that language ("le cœur"); and "today" (winter, 1657) it is a question of testifying in public that the five propositions do in fact express the doctrinal positions of Jansenius.

9. Ambiguity is defined in this way: "a sentence [s] is ambiguous if and only if [s] admits of (at least) two paraphrases, [t] and [u], that are not paraphrases of one another." Robert Blair Edlow, *Galen on Language and Ambiguity* (Leiden: E. J. Brill, 1977), p. 13.

10. In his *Age de l'éloquence* (Geneva: Droz, 1980), Marc Fumaroli insists on the fundamental status of proper use and reception of language. From the rhetorician Pierre Bertius he gleans the following: "Qu'elle [l'éloquence] disparaisse, le commerce s'évanouirait, les échanges techniques et intellectuels seraient anéantis, avec les cultes divins, les lois, les traités, les réunions ou l'on débat des affaires publiques et privées, les assemblées où l'on célèbre Dieu; chacun pour soi, réduit à la méditation solitaire, découvrirait son inassouvissement triste, séparé, misérable, semblable plutôt à un être endormi qu'éveillé, à un mort qu'un vivant [...] Car le discours (*oratio*) est le lien de la société, et s'il est retiré, celle-ci ne peut que se défaire, au point de rendre inévitable la disparition du genre humain" (pp. 18-19).

From Etienne Gilson, Fumaroli takes this wisdom: "Ce qui rend la société possible, c'est le langage. Dire que l'homme est un animal sociable et que c'est un animal parlant, c'est donc dire la même chose [...] Le reste est important, mais rien ne l'est autant que ce privilège humain du langage, grâce auquel les sociétés deviennent possibles, et avec leurs lois, leurs institutions, leurs arts, leurs sciences et leurs philosophies" (p. 42).

11. *Entendre* derives from the Latin verb *intendere* (to tend toward, to stretch).

12. "Il est clair que dans la religion aimable que les Jesuites rêvent d'instituer, la théorie de la grâce suffisante fait corps avec la morale relachée [...].

[...] Attaquer la grace suffisante c'est donc attaquer par avance la morale débonaire; attaquer la morale débonaire c'est ruiner la grâce suffisante" Albert Bayet *Les Provinciales de Pascal* (Paris: Société Française d'Editions Littéraires et Techniques, 1929), pp. 50-51.

Chapter Three

1. Marsha Reisler, "Persuasion through Antithesis: An Analysis of the Dominant Rhetorical Structure of Pascal's *Lettres provinciales*," *Romanic Review*, vol. 69, no. 3 (May 1978): 173.

2. The difference between exposé and response is an admittedly fine one and is drawn as much for practical, heuristic, and organizational reasons as it is to mark procedural and conceptual distinctions in Pascal's text.

3. See *Dictionnaire Robert*.

4. Philip Lewis, *op. cit.*, p. 33.

5. Roger Duchêne: *L'Imposture littéraire dans les Provinciales de Pascal* (Aix-en-Provence: Université de Provence, 1984).

6. Louis Cognet, *Le Jansénisme* (Paris: Presses Universitaires de France, 1961), p. 46.

7. Alain-Michel Boyer, "Les Ciseaux savent lire," *Revue des sciences humaines*, vol. 4 (1984): 107.

8. Antoine Compagnon writes of the quotation as a lure and a motivating agent: "Toute citation [...] est une leurre et une force motrice, son sens est dans l'accident ou dans le choc. L'analysant comme un fait de langage, il faut compter avec sa puissance et veiller à ne pas neutraliser celle-ci, car cette puissance phénoménale, ce pouvoir mobilisateur, c'est la citation telle qu'en elle-même avant d'être pour quelque chose." *La Seconde Main* (Paris: Editions du Seuil, 1979), p. 45.

9. "En vérité, lui dis-je, je trouvais tantôt à redire au procédé des Molinistes; mais après ce que vous m'avez dit, j'admire leur prudence et leur politique. Je vois bien qu'ils ne pouvaient rien faire de plus judicieux ni de plus sûr. Vous l'entendez, me dit-il: leur plus sûr parti a toujours été de se taire. Et c'est ce qui a fait dire à un savant théologien: Que les plus habiles d'entre eux sont ceux qui intriguent beaucoup, qui parlent peu et qui n'écrivent point" (Letter 3, pp. 58-59).

10. "Car ne voyons-nous pas que Dieu hait et méprise les pécheurs tout ensemble, jusque-là même qu'à l'heure de leur mort, qui est le temps où leur état est le plus déplorable et la plus triste, la sagesse divine joindra la moquerie et la risée à la vengeance et à la fureur qui les condamnera à des supplices éternels [...]?" (Letter 11, p. 149).

11. Cognet points out that Arnauld, who had used Tertullain's thought in his *Réponse à la lettre d'une personne de condition* (date...), translates "très exactement" his source. Pascal, on the other hand, is said to be "beaucoup plus loin de l'original," *Le Jansénisme*, p. 199.

12. "Et quoique je ne fasse que rapporter simplement et citer fidèlement leurs paroles, je ne sais néanmoins s'il ne se pourrait pas rencontrer quelque esprit bizarre qui, s'imaginant que cela vous fait tort, n'en tirât de vos principes quelque méchante conclusion" (Letter 7, pp. 107-08).

13. "Car, qu'y a-t-il de plus propre à exciter à rire que de voir une chose aussi grave que la morale chrétienne remplie d'imaginations aussi grotesque que les vôtres? On concoit une si haute attente de ces maxims, qu'on dit que JESUS-CHRIST *a lui-même révélées à des Pères de la Société, que* quand on y trouve *qu'un prêtre qui a reçu de l'argent pour dire une Messe peut, outre cela, en prendre d'autres personnes, en leur cédant toute sa part qu'il a au sacrifice; qu'un religieux n'est pas excommunié pour quitter son habit lorsque c'est pour danser, pour filouter, ou pour aller incognito en des lieux de débauche; et qu'on satisfait au précepte d'ouïr la messe en entendant quatre quarts de messe à la fois de différents prêtres* [...] (Letter 11, pp. 151-52).

14. "Je vous en parlerai peut-être quelque jour, mes Pères, et on sera surpris de voir combien vous êtes déchus du premier esprit de votre Institut, et que vos propres Généraux ont prévu que le dérèglement de votre doctrine dans la morale pourrait être funeste non seulement à votre Société, mais encore à l'Eglise universelle" (Letter 13, p. 185).

15. "Mais vous recherchez à dessein ces mots de *droit divin, droit positif, droit naturel, tribunal intérieur et extérieur, cas exprimés dans le droit, présomption externe,* et les autres qui sont peu connus, afin d'échapper sous cette obscurité, et de faire perdre la vue de vos égarements. Vous n'échapperez pas néanmoins, mes Pères, par ces vaines subtilités, car je vous ferai des questions si simples, qu'elles ne seront point sujettes au *distinguo* " (Letter 12, p. 168).

16. "Est-ce parler avec sincérité? Non, mes Pères, puisque vos réponses s'entre-détruisent" (Letter 15, p. 208).

Chapter Four

1. Henri Lefebvre. *Pascal* (Paris: Editions Nagel, 1949), p. 83.

2. "L'exigence d'univocité se définit essentiellement par négation: elle est la qualité de ce qui n'est pas équivoque. Et le mot 'équivoque' est l'un des plus importants au XVIIe siècle. Vaugelas, dans sa préface aux *Remarques sur la langue française* (1647), observe qu'il n'y a pas de langue 'qui soit plus ennemie des équivoques' que la nôtre." Edouard Morot-Sir, *La Métaphysique de Pascal* (Paris: Presses Universitaires de France, 1973), p. 15.

3. Jacques Derrida, "La Double Séance" in *La Dissemination* (Paris: Editions du Seuil, 1972), p. 219.

4. Heinrich Fries, *Revelation* (New York: Herder and Herder, 1969), p. 20.

5. Charles Journet writes of revelation as the "proposition extérieure et manifeste" and as "la vérité à croire et la vérité à faire." *La Message révélé* (Paris: Desclée de Brouwer, 1964), p. 7.

6. Paul Bénichou underscores the fundamental devalorisation of human values characteristic of the Jansenist world view: "La théologie janséniste est destinée à écraser, non pas le matérialisme, mais plutôt toute forme de spiritualisme, même chrétien, qui ne

s'accompagne pas d'une négation absolue des valeurs humaines, toute forme de vertu ou de grandeur suspecte de practiser avec la nature et avec l'instinct." *Morales du grand siècle* (Paris: Gallimard, 1948), p. 127.

7. Harold Alderman, "Heidegger's Critique of Science and Technology," in *Heidegger and Modern Philosophy*, ed. Michael Murray (New Haven: Yale University Press, 1978), pp. 37-38.

8. "C'est cette partie dominante dans l'homme, cette maîtresse d'erreur et de fausseté, et d'autant plus fourbe qu'elle ne l'est pas toujours; car elle serait règle infaillible de vérité, si elle l'était infaillible du mensonge. Mais étant le plus souvent fausse, elle ne donne aucune marque de sa qualité, marquant du même caractère le vrai et le faux."

9. This observation, which appears at the very end of Letter 13, serves to turn the logic of Scripture, of the "esprit de Dieu" literally against the numerologic that would provide for a multiplicity of "voies," which are the ways and means of avoiding the demands of the heart.

10. Bénichou, *op. cit.*, p. 147.

11. See *Cassell's Latin-English Dictionary*.

12. Along with the desire for the salvation of those against whom one speaks, the "spirit of charity" would oblige one to "adresser ses prières à Dieu en même temps qu'on adresse ses reproches aux hommes" (p. 156).

13. "C'est une chose étrange, mes Pères, qu'on ait néanmoins de quoi vous convaincre que, votre haine contre vos adversaires ayant été jusqu'à souhaiter leur perte éternelle, votre aveuglement ait été jusqu'à découvrir un souhait si abominable; que bien loin de former en secret des désirs de leur salut, vous avez fait en public des vœux pour leur damnation [...]" (Letter 11, p. 159).

14. A perfect example of the self-destructive nature of the casuist project is laid out in Letter 6. Jean d'Alba, an employee of the Jesuits themselves at their Collège de Clermont (the present day Lycée Louis le Grand), convinced that he was not being paid a sufficient wage, pilfered some pewter tableware from his employers. Brought to trial for petty thievery, Alba, apparently up to date on the casuist codes, argued his case by appealing to a maxim by Bauny which stipulates that an employee may supplement his wages if he feels he should be earning more.

15. "La volonté, dans l'humanité déchue, étant dominée par la concupiscence, qui l'empêche de se tourner vers Dieu, et la tient constamment tournée vers la créature, c'est-à-dire, en dernière analyse, vers elle-même, cette sorte de maladie de l'attention fait que, partout où la concupiscence est en cause, l'amour-propre nous aveugle. [...]

Lui non plus ne conteste pas la puissance de la raison humaine en matière de 'sciences abstraites,' mathématique et physique. Mais il croit cette raison à peu près totalement impuissante en matière de métaphysique et en matière de morale—les deux choses, d'ailleurs, étant à ses yeux connexes." Jean Laporte, *Le Cœur et la raison selon Pascal* (Paris: Elzévir, 1950), pp. 16-17.

Bibliography

Adam, Antoine. *Du Mysticism à la révolte: les Jansénistes au dix-septième siècle.* Paris: Fayrad, 1968.

Alderman, Harold. "Heidegger's Critique of Science and Technology," in *Heidegger and Modern Philosophy*, ed. Michael Murray. New Haven: Yale University Press, 1978.

Alquié, Ferdinand. "Pascal et la critique moderne." *Critique* 126 (1957): 953-67.

Arnould, Auguste. *Les Jésuites depuis leur origine jusqu'à nos jours.* Paris: Michel Levy, 1846.

Austin, J. L. *How To Do Things with Words.* Cambridge: Harvard University Press, 1962.

Bayet, Albert. *Les Provinciales de Pascal.* Paris: Société française d'Editions Littéraires et Techniques, 1929.

Bénichou, Paul. *Morales du grand siècle.* Paris: Gallimard, 1948.

Berlin, Isaiah. et. al. *Essays on J. L. Austin.* Oxford: Clarendon Press, 1973.

Boyer, Alain-Michel. "Les Ciseaux savent lire." *Revue des sciences humaines*, 4 (1984): 107-17.

Bréhier, Emile. *The History of Philosophy. The Seventeenth Century*, translation by Wade Baskin. Chicago: University of Chicago Press, 1966.

Brémond, Henri. *Histoire littéraire du sentiment religieux en France*, tome 1. Paris: Armand Colin, 1967.

Chaix-Ruy, Jules. *Le Jansénisme et Port-Royal.* Paris: Feliz-Alcan, 1930.

Cognet, Louis. *Le Jansénisme.* Paris: Presses Universitaires de France, 1961.

Compagnon, Antoine. *La seconde main.* Paris: Editions du Seuil, 1979.

Daniel-Rops, Henri. *L'Eglise des temps classiques.* Paris: Fayard, 1958.

Davidson, Hugh. *Audience, Words and Art.* Columbus: Ohio State University Press, 1965.

———. *Blaise Pascal.* Boston: Twayne World Authors Series, 1983.

Davidson, Hugh and Dubé, Pierre. *A Concordance to Pascal's Lettres Provinciales.* New York: Garland, 1980.

Demorest, Jean-Jacques. *Dans Pascal.* Paris: Editions de Minuit, 1953.

Derrida, Jacques. *La Dissemination.* Paris: Editions du Seuil, 1972.

————— *Positions*. Paris: Editions du Seuil, 1972.

Duchêne, Roger. *L'Imposture littéraire dans les Provinciales de Pascal*. Aix-en-Provence: Université de Provence, 1984.

Edlow, Robert Blair. *Galen on Language and Ambiguity*. Leiden: E. J. Brill, 1977.

Ferreyrolles, Gérard. *Blaise Pascal: Les Provinciales* . Paris: Presses Universitaires de France, 1984.

Fries, Heinrich. *Revelation*. New York: Herder and Herder, 1969.

Fumaroli, Marc. *Age de l'éloquence*. Geneva: Droz, 1980.

Gazier, Augustin. *Histoire générale du mouvement janséniste*. Paris: Honoré Champion, 1922.

Goldmann, Lucien. *Le Dieu caché*. Paris: Gallimard, 1955.

James, E. D. "The Problems of Sufficient Grace in the *Lettres Provinciales*." *French Studies*, 21, 3 (1967): 205-19.

Journet, Charles. *Le Message révélé*. Paris: Desclée de Brouwer, 1964.

Krailsheimer, Alban. *Pascal*. New York: Hill and Wang, 1980.

Kuentz, P. "Un Discours nommé Montalte." *Revue d'Histoire Littéraire de la France*, 71, 2 (1971): 195-206.

Laporte, Jean. *Le Cœur et la raison selon Pascal*. Paris: Elzévir, 1950.

LeBrun, François. *Le XVII siècle*. Paris: Armand Colin, 1967.

Lefebvre, Henri. *Pascal*. Paris: Editions Nagel, 1949.

Lewis, Philip. "Dialogic Impasse in Pascal's *Provinciales*." Canadian Review of Comparative Literature, Winter (1976): 27-38.

Marin, Louis. "Pascal: Text, Author, Discourse...." *Yale French Studies*, 52 (1975): 129-51.

Mesnard, Jean. *Pascal*. Paris: Desclée de Brouwer, 1965.

Miel, Jan. *Pascal and Theology*. Baltimore: Johns Hopkins University Press, 1969.

Morot-Sir, Edouard. *La Métaphysique de Pascal*. Paris: Presses Universitaires de France, 1977.

Nelson, Robert. *Pascal: Adversary and Advocate*. Cambridge: Harvard University Press, 1981.

Pascal, Blaise. *Lettres écrites à un provincial*. Ed. Antoine Adam. Paris: Garnier-Flammarion, 1981.

————. *Œuvres complètes*. Ed. Louis Lafuma. Paris: Editions du Seuil, 1963.

————. *Les Provinciales*. Ed. Louis Cognet. Paris: Garnier Frères, 1965.

Rapin, René. *Mémoires [...] sur l'Eglise et la société, la cour, la ville et le jansénisme, 1644-1699*. Paris: Gaume Frères, 1865.

Reisler, Marsha. "Persuasion through Antithesis: An Analysis of the Dominant Rhetorical Structure of Pascal's *Lettres provinciales*." *Romanic Review*, 69 (1978): 172-85.

Rex, Walter. *Pascal's Provincial Letters: An Introduction*. London: Hodder and Staughton, 1977.

Russier, Jeanne. *La Foi selon Pascal*. Paris: Presses Universitaires de France, 1949.

Sainte-Beuve. *Port-Royal*. Paris: Pléiade, 1952.

Saint-Gilles. *Journal*, Ed. Ernest Jovy. Paris: J. Vrin, 1936.

Sedgwick, Alexander. *Jansenism in Seventeenth-Century France: Voices in the Wilderness*. Charlottesville: University of Virginia Press, 1977.

Sellier, Philippe. *Pascal et Saint Augustin*. Paris: Armand Colin, 1970.

Shea, William D. "L'Antithèse clarté-obscurité dans la 12e Provinciale." *Romance Notes*, 13 (1971-72): 314-17.

Slights, William W. E. "Pattern and Persona in Pascal's *Lettres Provinciales*." *Kentucky Romance Quarterly*, 14, 2 (1967): 126-38.

Steinmann, Jean. *Pascal*. Paris: Desclée de Brouwer, 1962.

Topliss, Patricia. *The Rhetoric of Pascal*. Amsterdam: Leicester University Press, 1966.

Weber, Joseph. "Person as Figure of Ambiguity and Resolution in Pascal." *PMLA*, 84 (1969): 312-20.